RIVERBOAT LANDING
A History of the Ocklawaha River Steamboats
Authors
Michael C. Mason Edward A. Mueller

Dedication and Thank You

This book is dedicated to William Carl Mason, my grandfather, and Franklin W. Mason, my father, whose lives have been influenced by their involvement of working, living, and growing up near the river. As I grew up my father constantly educated me about the river and its far-reaching effects and uniqueness. I am very fortunate to have had a mentor who instilled in me the importance of passing along this valuable information.

For over 30 years, I have dreamed of producing a book of information with full-color images of the

Ocklawaha River and the Riverboats that plied it. Over the years, as my knowledge grew I realized that tourism was not the only aspect of commerce on the river. It also included the turpentine, citrus, logging, and lumbering industries.

My interest started during my upbringing while being constantly taught by my grandfather and father about the importance of the history of the river. I wished to preserve this valuable knowledge, which might otherwise have been lost, not only for my daughter, Cynthia, but others of her generation.

A special thank you goes to Edward A. Mueller. He and I have been friends for the past 25 years, and I have gained much knowledge from him about the River and the Steamboat Era. His book *Ocklawaha River Steamboats* was known as the most complete informational guide on the Ocklawaha River and its steamboats, and when I approached him about including its information in my book, he agreed and he wished me well.

My biggest thanks of all is to my mother, without her postcard collection, which she gathered over the past sixty plus years, many of the images you see in this book might not have been available. Also, I wish to thank my brother, Dale, and daughter, Cynthia, for their continued support on this project.

A special thanks to Paula Racey and W. Dale Smith on the creation and production of the book. Without their dedication and many hours of hard work, it would not have been possible.

And finally, my sincere thanks to the staff at E. O. Painter Printing Company, in DeLeon Springs, Florida, for all their printing expertise.

Michael C. Mason
Publisher/Editor

Foreword

August, 1997

Ocklawaha River Steamboats has gone through two printings and is now out of print. There seems to be continued demand for this book, so the author resolved to reprint it, but at the same time, take advantage of better technology and some new material. Revising the volume also permitted several typographical errors to be corrected and a few errors of fact changed. So the reader will find that all the previous material has been carefully reviewed, some new print fonts have been used, several photos added, and a better publication thereby produced. The original foreword also has been changed to bring material up to the 1997 year.

Over four decades ago, the author was fortunate to make the acquaintance of, and develop a friendship with, C. Bradford Mitchell. "Brad", as his friends knew him, exposed the author to his comprehensive treatise on Ocklawaha River Steamboats, *Paddle-Wheel Inboard*, which appeared in two consecutive issues of the *American Neptune* quarterly in 1947. This highly respected quarterly had a limited circulation in Florida and very few knew of it. Of course, it has been long out of print.

At the author's request, Mr. Mitchell has set forth an account of how *Paddle-Wheel Inboard* came into being. In his words:

"ON FINDING BURIED TREASURE—AND LOSING IT

"War, by universal consensus, is hell. Hence, any blessing it may inadvertently confer is memorable. Thus it was for my wife Louise in the late winter of 1943 when, driving north after leaving me at a South Florida installation of the Army Air Forces Technical Training Command, she took shelter from a tropical storm at a tourist court on Hart's Point, across the St. Johns River from Palatka. Unwittingly, she had stumbled—or splashed—into history.

"While the storm blew itself out she learned from her hosts, Mr. and Mrs. P. W. Thompson, that they were the current heirs to, and custodians of, what remained of the Ocklawaha River steamboat service established by Hubbard L. Hart before the Civil War and carried on by an elder generation of Thompons until the end

of the First World War. Adjoining the tourist court, she was shown Hart's orange grove and former shipyard, including the decaying hulk of HIAWATHA, his line's last steamer. In Palatka the Thompsons lived in the brick riverfront block which still housed the Hart Line office and a large collection of records, pictures, and artifacts which the Thompsons hoped ultimately to preserve in a museum on board a reconditioned HIAWATHA.

"But first there was a war to outlast. Not until January, 1946, was it possible to accept the Thompsons' invitation to return together and explore their holdings. This we did for a dreary succession of such days as only the South can produce in winter, in a damp, unheated room practically overhanging the river. The rewards, however, more than offset the inconvenience of wearing overcoats and gloves (despite an electric heater kindly loaned by the Thompsons). For here, thoroughly jumbled, was the full life story of a unique riverboat operation.

"A sketchy census of the Thompson holdings taken in the course of sorting and excerpting the most significant, showed them to consist, first, of correspondence (99% longhand and 90% scrawl) between Hart, his personal and official families, patrons of his line, politicians, competitors, and various friends and backwoods entrepreneurs. Second, there were voluminous financial and statistical data: bills, repair yard accounts, passenger and freight ledgers. Third, there was a large, relatively complete series of colored Hart Line schedule cards, each with a timetable, a standard woodcut of a steamer (usually OKEEHUMKEE), and often a route map. A fourth major category was pictures—primarily several hundred stereopticon photographs, one hundred of which we luckily preserved in negative copies.

"Even with both of us working long days for the full week which was all we had, it was obviously possible only to skim the cream of this material and to assemble enough highlight notes to be later expanded into an outline history. When this was published the next year, under the title *Paddle-Wheel Inboard*, it was with the hope we might soon return to Palatka for research in greater depths—or that some scholar would be prompted by reading it to do so. Neither happened. By the time retirement allowed a reopening of the subject, the HIAWATHA was gone and no certain information was available as to the fate of the Hart-Thompson records.

"In long retrospect, it is a good thing that an outline history, at least, was published—and an even better thing that scholars such as Ed Mueller are still pursuing the Ocklawaha story.

-C. Bradford Mitchell"

Mr. Mitchell for many years was editor of *Steamboat Bill*, the quarterly publication (some say Bible) of the Steamship Historical Society of America, an organization that he also helped to found. An avid helper of the Society was the late Mr. R. Loren Graham, who was instrumental in getting fine steamboat photos copied for posterity. Mr. Graham copied many photos of Ocklawaha River steamboats loaned by the Thompsons, most of which appeared in a reduced form in the *American Neptune* series of articles. Later on, Mr. Mitchell gave the copy negatives to the author, and they have been the start of his collection of Ocklawaha materials, which now number in the hundreds of items.

For over 30 years, the author has sporadically collected Ocklawaha material such as references, photos, clippings, and information by means of interviews with descendants of old time river personages. The author has a hobby (rather an avocation or obsession) of collecting written and pictorial materials on Florida-based steamboats and has previously concentrated his efforts on rivers such as the St. Johns, Apalachicola, Suwannee, Kissimmee and the like.

In 1982, the author decided to produce a definitive photo-oriented book on the Ocklawaha River steamboats, and the original and second printings were the results.

The author acknowledges his gratitude and kind thanks to the late Brad Mitchell for the fine materials he produced and the summaries and notes used in producing *Paddle-Wheel Inboard*, all of which were made available and a considerable amount used in this book. Mr. Mitchell concentrated on Colonel Hubbard L. Hart and his efforts. The author has located other materials, especially about Hart's competitors, notably Captain Henry Gray, S. J. Bouknight and Captain J. Hatten Howard, and these pages reflect that knowledge.

The author was introduced to the venerable HIAWATHA in 1956 by his fellow traffic engineer, the late Henry Boggs. Even at that time, 41 years ago, it was but a forgotten ruin; many people in Palatka, for example, were not even aware that it was an Ocklawaha craft. Henry Boggs also saw to it that the author participated in a most interesting boat-a-cade from Welaka to Silver Springs on a delightful Saturday in the late-1950s.

Shortly after the first printing had been accomplished, Mrs. Caroline Wellhoner Farmer of Silver Springs brought the author's attention to her grandfather's line, The Mills Line, and details of it follow in the narrative section.

Over the years, the author has corresponded and collected in a desultory fashion, and has gradually accumulated enough materials for the formulation of this book.

The author wishes to acknowledge the help of Captain Henry Gray's descendants, Mrs. Ola Kane of East Palatka, Mrs. Nancy Dorsett of Hilton Head, South Carolina, and Mrs. Mary Sweeney of El Paso, Texas. All were kind enough to loan pictorial and written materials.

Others in Palatka such as Cody Merwin, Mary Gale, Mary Murphy, and Roger Stumbo, all of the Putnam County Historical Society, and many others, such as Corben Sapp, lent encouragement or materials. An especial debt is owed Norma Bennett of Interlachen for her constant encouragement and enthusiasm for this project and others such as "Henrietta" that she has in mind.

Don Chapman of Orange Springs offered continual support. Robert Cauthen of Leesburg helped by loan of key materials, and Norma Hendricks, Miriam W. Johnson and "Brownie" Brownsberger, all of the Lake County, Florida, Historical Society, have been helpful. Doug Hendricksen of Merritt Island loaned key photographs. Storm Richards of Sanford was helpful with his study. The late N. Clement "Clem" Slade of Jacksonville provided several stereo photographs. John Palmer of Interlachen found many helpful photos. Al Robson also furnished photographs. Frank Manwell was of great help.

The author owes a significant debt of gratitude to Mrs. Allen (Joan) Morris, photo archivist at the Florida Photographic Archives, now housed at the

Florida Department of State's archives, and her husband Allen. Mrs. Morris substantially enhanced the author's collection and knowledge. Her husband, Allen Morris, had started the state's photographic collection many years ago and saw it safely installed at the Florida State University Library in its infancy and formative period. By the work of the Morrises, copies of many hundreds of contemporary photographs are being preserved and subsequently made available for historians of the future.

The Museum of Florida History, Division of Archives, History and Records Management, Department of State, was especially helpful in providing access to key materials. Their steamboat exhibit project was focused on the Ocklawaha River and Silver Springs. Helpful and cooperative staff there at that time included Patricia R. Wickman, Historian, John LoCastro, Exhibit Designer, and Ed Jonas, Exhibit Designer.

Perhaps the most substantial debt must be paid to a group of virtually unknown persons, the stereo photographers of the 1870s, 80s and 90s. Coming to Florida from the north for the most part, they spent their winters photographing the Ocklawaha River and its environs and often its steamboats.

Most are nameless and they sold their negatives or photos to publishers of photographic series on the river or published their materials without claiming authorship. However, Charles Seaver, Jr. emerges as one of this group as does George Barker. The latter's known photos are fewer than others, but those found are of sterling quality even as measured by today's standards. Several of Seaver's and Barker's photos appear in these pages.

Then as now the tourist arriving at Silver Springs and gazing on its wonders, found time to pause for a moment in time and was duly recorded. Many of these photos appear in these pages, and it is a wonder that they have come through a century relatively unscathed. These photos were sold to the tourists on each trip, and Colonel Hart saved all the unsold ones; hence some are still available, as the Colonel was not one to throw away that which could be saved.

The steamboat period of the Ocklawaha lasted about six decades. A few individuals served to foster it and keep it alive—and on a river that offered more than its degree of challenge, having as it does more turns by far than it has miles. The narrative that accompanies this photographic presentation singles out those hardy entrepreneurs and captains for which records can be found.

Captain J. Hatten Howard, II, owner of the WILLIAM HOWARD, is the only master that operated on the river that the author was privileged to meet. Some 35 years ago, the author met him at his Daytona Beach Chris Craft business, and Captain Howard indicated what he remembered and loaned several photos. An article by Captain Howard and his experiences appear in these pages.

The author is also indebted to Cathy Chaplin for her help in the original composition and to Rev. John Buchheimer, Pastor of Bethlehem Lutheran Church in Jacksonville Beach for his help in lettering on the cover and other headings. Brad Mitchell was kind enough to review and critique the original history. Joyce Fitzpatrick was kind enough to perform the same task for this account.

Also pleasant to relate is the fact that the Steamship Historical Society of America has reprinted Brad's articles as a separate publication that makes a good companion to this volume.

The exact title of the reprint is "*Paddle-Wheel Inboard: Some of the History of Ocklawaha River Steamboating and of the Hart Line (American Neptune*, 1947; reissued 1983; Steamship Historical Society of America)."

Because this publication concentrates on steamboats, vessel names are capitalized for special emphasis, even in quoted material. This deviation from normal practice is similar to that employed in *Steamboat Bill*, official publication of the Steamship Historical Society of America.

Mrs. Caroline Wellhoner Farmer was kind enough to inform the author of her grandfather's river service, the Mills Line, and that brief account has been added. Thanks to her for the information and pictorial materials furnished.

General Ulysses Grant's 1880 visit to Florida—A trip on the Ocklawaha on the OSCEOLA.

TABLE OF CONTENTS
Part 1

Ocklawaha River Steamboats

The expression, "A weird trip up a gloomy and amazing river," characterizes the steamboat era on the Ocklawaha River.[1] Six decades of steam-propelled travel were to occur, decades that would see some of the most unusual vessels ever to traverse inland waters. Known (in its time) as a major tourist destination for the Florida visitor, the river is now plied by pleasure boats ranging from canoes to small craft on fishing expeditions to powerful cruisers. Ever a tortuous and crooked river that slowed a vessel to a crawl, the journey was worth the scenery viewed and the usual reward at its end, a visit to Silver Springs.

This river, now usually spelled Oklawaha, but in steamboat times, Ocklawaha (which name is used in this story), has its source in the system of large lakes (Griffin, Eustis, Dora, Harris and Apopka) in the central area of the peninsula of Florida, and flows northerly, then eastwardly, emptying into the St. Johns River in the vicinity of Welaka, some 22 miles south of Palatka.

The extreme head of the system may be taken as Lake Apopka, 120 miles (distances according to the U.S. Engineers) above the mouth of the river. The width is from 50 to 200 feet in the lower portion and up to 75 feet above Silver Springs Run, a large tributary which enters 53 miles above the mouth. The stream has a fall of about 0.7 feet per mile and a moderately rapid current. The drainage area is about 750 square miles. The discharge is about 800 "second feet" at ordinary stages below Silver Springs Run and 125 "second feet" at low water above Silver Springs Run. Low stages occur from March to September.[2]

In the mid-nineteenth century, the Ocklawaha was obstructed by logs, snags, overhanging trees, and accumulations of drift and aquatic vegetation. Navigation was impeded by all of the above in addition to narrow places and sharp bends in the river. The controlling depth was 3.5 to 4 feet from the mouth to Silver Springs Run and about 2 feet from there to Lake Griffin. The channel width varied from 22 to 175 feet.

Leesburg, at the head of Lake Griffin, 94 miles above the mouth, was generally regarded as the head of navigation, but light-draft steamboats and launches could pass through the lakes and connecting creeks and canals as far as Lake Apopka.[3]

As early as 1835, Congress saw the need for improving the river and made its first provision to this end on February 24th of that year.[4] Most of the improvements for steamboat purposes were made by the state of Florida, because of the reluctance of the federal government to furnish the funds during the time needed. Long after the cessation of any steamboat travel, the federal government attempted to revive navigation by the proposed, then started, but not-to-be-completed Florida Cross State Barge Canal. This canal used the Ocklawaha for a considerable distance, and before the project was stopped, a considerable length of the lower river was dammed up. A new junction with the St. Johns River was created to the north of the natural junction.

The story of the river navigation can be divided into several stages or eras. Early activities are largely unrecorded until just before Civil War days but were certainly minimal. Some of the stages that will be covered in the following pages are:

- The Second Seminole Indian War and related steamboat activity, 1835 - 1842.

- Early river activity including rafting and the use of pole barges.

- Civil War days and blockade running.

- Postwar navigation improvements.

- The dominance of the Hart Line for 25 years.

- The competitive era of the 1890s.

- The declining days of the 1910s.

- The emergence of gasoline-powered craft in the 1910s and the 1920s.

- End of steamboat activity.

In the first third of the nineteenth century, the state was sparsely populated. Largely unknown and somewhat unexplored below the area of present-day Orlando, the rivers, coastal waterways and areas near the ocean were the centers of population. Northern Florida had an agricultural economy and comprised most of the Florida that was settled.

The first steamboats visited Florida in 1829 and were on the St. Johns and the Apalachicola rivers. Regular service was established on the St. Johns in the early 1830s, and the outbreak of the Second Seminole Indian War in December of 1835 stimulated much activity as steamboats were employed to fulfill the logistical supply needs of the troops battling the elusive Seminoles. During the 1835-42 war period, thousands of passages were made to and from Florida by steam-propelled vessels. Very few of these ever penetrated the Ocklawaha although Fort Brooke, some 32 river miles from the mouth, was established and undoubtedly supplied by water.

After the war, efforts were increased to attract more settlers (including using land grants as bounties for war veterans). Travel to and within the state was largely by water and steamships and steamboats provided much of the service. Palatka was the normal head of navigation for steamboats using the St. Johns River, and service from Savannah was offered in the mid-1830s on a more or less regular basis, although often interrupted by wartime operations.

In the early 1850s, service was offered from Charleston, and several craft were running on the St. Johns from Jacksonville to Enterprise and Mellonville, both on Lake Monroe. Of course, the advent of the Civil War and the Union invasions of the St. Johns area brought most of this steamboat traffic to a close.

One of the after-effects of the Seminole War was the provision of land grants which were given as bonuses or bounties to participants in the conflict. This stimulated immigration, and greater reliance was placed on that aid to the development of Florida, the steamboat. By the 1850s, settlement was increasing on both coasts of the state and along the St. Johns.

Pre-steamboat waterborne activity on the Ocklawaha was largely related to logging and the lumber industry. Trees were cut along the river, made into logs which were placed together in rafts and then floated down to the St. Johns. They were transported to Jacksonville and were processed into lumber at the many sawmills and then loaded aboard sailing vessels for destinations along the eastern seaboard and abroad. Cedar was an especially valued lumber and cypress was plentiful, both are scarce today. In time Southern yellow pine would be a huge export.

Barges powered by poling were the first commercial vessels on the river. The laden barges would carry merchandise upstream and products of the region downstream to market. The pole barge operations usually originated at Palatka and ended at a point on the Ocklawaha determined by water depth and demand. The barges were propelled by a gang of men, often slaves in pre-war days, each equipped with a pole. This would be placed in the water at the bow, and the crew member would walk to the stern, pushing on the pole as he went. Arriving at the stern, the next man picked up the pole, walked to the bow and placed the pole in the water again, repeating the man-killing process endlessly. The poles were also used to push the barge away from the riverbanks.

About three weeks was required for the round trip between Palatka and Silver Springs. Although the work was laborious and time-consuming, the small settlements near the river provided some sort of trade for the barges which continued for several years.

The lands bordering on the Ocklawaha are mostly swamp-like, but occasional patches of high ground broke through the cypress swamp and served as landings for the boats and as avenues to the interior. Many of these landings had crude piers or wharves, and, usually, a small shed was provided nearby to protect goods and passengers from the weather.

The river is divided into two principal parts. The first, and the most significant from a steamboat viewpoint, was from Silver Springs Run (also known as the Silver River) to the mouth of the Ocklawaha at the St. Johns River, slightly south of Welaka. The other part is from Silver Springs Run to Lake Griffin. A shallower part of the river, it was less and less frequented by steamboats as time went on. A common feature of both sections was the tortuous, always twisting path of the river.

Silver Springs, then as now an "attraction", was the principal destination of the travelers who braved the Ocklawaha one hundred and forty years ago. Daniel Brinton was one of the first to bring the "glories" of Silver Springs to the attention of the world and recorded his observations in 1859.[5] He asserted, "to be appreciated in its full beauty it should be approached from the Ockleweha (sic)." He had taken more than a week traversing the 'dark and crooked river' in a pole barge, "wearied with the monotony of the dark and gloomy forests that everywhere shade its inky stream, when one bright morning a sharp turn brought us into the pellucid waters of the Silver Springs Run."[6]

The initial direct references to boats on the river occur in the mid-1850s. In August of 1854, the barge OCKLAWAHA was launched at the Jacksonville shipyard of J. C. Butler. She was designated to ply on the river of her name from Welaka to Silver Springs.[7] Another vessel, the FAWN, was launched in February, 1855. She was built by John Clark, an area pioneer and a respected merchant of Jacksonville who was also a steamboat owner and agent. No official document has been found and the FAWN may never have been officially enrolled. She had a hull about 52 feet long and was 10 feet wide. Her length at deck level was about 56 feet and she had a 10 horsepower engine. Her owner was J. C. Bryant, a local lawyer, who observed the launching by a speech. Captain Louis Mitchell Coxetter, master of the Charleston-based CAROLINA which ran to Florida, and perhaps the best-known steamboat man of the time, christened her.

In 1859, a small steamboat was being built in Palatka. She was the GENERAL or, more correctly, the GENERAL SUMTER, 81 feet long by 19 feet wide by 3 feet depth of hold. She was of 42 tons. Completed in January 1860. Joseph Gallagher was her principal captain and James Devall of Palatka, her owner. Her career is little known but she was captured by the federal vessel COLUMBINE during the Civil War. The GENERAL SUMTER may have plied the lower part of the Ocklawaha river.

The early years of steamboating on the river immediately before the Civil War saw two entrepreneurs emerge as prominent personalities. They were Hubbard L. Hart and Henry Alexander Gray.

Hubbard L. Hart, developer and proprietor of the Hart Line of Ocklawaha River vessels, was born in Guildford, Windham County, Vermont, on May 4, 1827. His early life was spent on a farm there. He attended area grammar and high schools. When he was 21 years old, he came south in search of a business opportunity and spent three winters visiting various places along the Atlantic Coast, even venturing to Cuba. In 1852, he settled in Savannah, where he purchased the stage line that carried the U.S. Mail between there and Darien, Georgia. He managed this line for three years, but longing for a better opportunity, disposed of his interest, and moved to Florida.

On July 1, 1855, he opened a stage line between Palatka and Tampa. According to W. A. Pratt, Hart was supposedly in the last stages of consumption at the time of his arrival in Palatka but "recovered by his own efforts and the help of the climate." He became a powerful man physically and was always an active business man.

In 1860 he brought wharf property at Palatka and began a forwarding, receiving and shipping business, in conjunction with which he ran a general store.[8]

Captain Henry Alexander Gray was a captain in two ways, as an Ocklawaha River steamboat master and as an officer in the Confederate Army. A pioneer in the Ocklawaha trade, he served as owner or captain all of his life.

Captain Gray was born in Tattnall County, Georgia, on December 18, 1826, and after 16 years' residence there, went to Savannah and started working on a Savannah River steamboat. After two years of this activity he bought a mule and set off for Florida via his ancestral home in Tattnall County. An uncle persuaded him to trade the mule for a small yellow-colored horse, and Henry Gray rode the animal to Ellaville, Florida, on the Suwannee River.

In Ellaville he found a job on a Suwannee River steamboat plying to Cedar Keys. When he had completed several years' service he was promoted to captain. About 1849-50, after holding this position for some time, he had the unfortunate experience of running his steamboat into a high rocky bank of the river, tearing out one of his sidewheels. This cost him the position of captain.

With the intention of going to California for the gold rush, Captain Gray journeyed to Cedar Keys to get on a schooner bound for New Orleans. While waiting there he chanced upon a Frenchman who interested him in a large trace of cedar timber located on Star Island in the Ocklawaha River. Star Island is 98 miles from Palatka by the St. Johns and Ocklawaha rivers and 37 miles below Silver Springs. The tract was available for purchase and, if the cedar could be brought to market, would offer a sizeable financial reward.

The two decided to investigate the opportunity and started to walk to Ocala, walking being the only direct means to get there. Captain Gray had $1,500 in gold and carried it around his waist in a leather money belt. He also had a small rifle with which to kill game for food en route. At night the two would sleep in the woods, using moss pulled down from the trees as bedding.

This "roughing it" gave Captain Gray a bad fever and touches of rheumatism. Arriving at Ocala, he secured accommodations at the home of Mrs. Emma White who nursed him through three weeks of serious illness. After he recovered, Gray and his partner bought the cedar tract and, equipping themselves with food, lumbering equipment and supplies, went to Silver Springs and then downriver to Star Island, and the logging commenced. The cedar was cut, squared off into logs which were made into rafts, and then the rafts were floated or "poled" downstream to Welaka on the St. Johns, opposite the mouth of the Ocklawaha, some 72 miles as the river flows. There the cedar logs were loaded on schooners and carried to Savannah where they were sold. Several such cedar rafts were made and floated and sold, and a goodly sum of money realized.

The two partners separated after the cedar had been cut. Henry Gray went to Palatka and started in the business of trading to Silver Springs. Buying several slaves, he opened a pole barge line between Palatka and the Springs. Pole barging was laborious, but good profits could be made. Merchandise was carried on the upbound trip for the small settlements of Orange Springs, Micanopy, Ocala

and Leesburg. The downbound trip saw cargoes of cotton, cedar and other lumber being brought to Palatka and transferred to northbound schooners and steamboats plying the St. Johns. In the early 1850s, a Gray family legend has it that Captain Gray operated one MICANOPY. A MICANOPY, of 37 tons, was built in Charleston in 1853 and was documented until 1855, but that seems to be the extent of knowledge about this vessel. The vessel was apparently named after a Seminole Indian chief.

In 1857, Captain Gray married Eliza Waddell on April 2. Eleven children were to result from this marriage, of which four were to die before the age of seven years.

Eliza Waddell was born on November 8, 1838, at Carrollton, Alabama, and moved to Columbia, South Carolina. At the age of 14 she left there and came to Palatka, to live there more or less permanently.[9]

In 1860, Hart bought the JAMES BURT.[10] Little is known of her, but she was probably smaller than the Palatka-built GENERAL SUMTER. She served an unknown length of time on the Ocklawaha River, and inaugurated Hart's service.

Hart's next vessel was the SILVER SPRING (Official Number 23066, 73.91 tons).[11] Little is known about this vessel either, but she did survive the Civil War and helped in restoring service after the conflict.

Captain Gray bought a steamboat which he named EMMA WHITE in honor of his Ocala friend. He operated this steamer between Palatka and Silver Springs in passenger and freight service as the Civil War came to Florida. No details are known of the EMMA WHITE except that she was a sternwheeler.[12]

Gray's EMMA WHITE was a casualty of the war. Supposedly the Confederates seized her and sank her across a low water point, the "bar" of the St. Johns River at Lake George, in an only partially successful attempt to block the river against federal vessel passage further upstream.

Hubbard L. Hart bought the remains of the EMMA WHITE after the conflict. The machinery of the EMMA WHITE was apparently removed before she was sunk, and Hart may have used it in one of his subsequent vessels as it was included in the purchase.[13]

For the initial phase of the war, before the event touched Florida, Hart plied the Ocklawaha and perhaps the St. Johns with his two vessels, the JAMES BURT and the SILVER SPRING. Hart's friend and employee, George Allen, was the captain of the SILVER SPRING.

The war in Florida started at Fernandina in 1862 with the federal invasion and later spread to the St. Johns region. Hart evacuated Mrs. Hart and their daughter to Orange Springs on Orange Creek, a tributary of the Ocklawaha, and a place of refuge during the war for displaced civilians. Despite being a Vermonter by birth, Hart and most of his northern born neighbors aligned themselves with the South.

Captain Gray politically was an old-line Whig, and he opposed the secession of Florida from the Union. However, after failing to respond to the first calls for volunteers, he later organized and drilled a company of home guards termed the St. Johns Rangers. This group was finally mustered in as Company B, Second Florida Cavalry, General Hopkins being the commander. Initially a First Lieutenant, Gray later achieved a captaincy and held this rank until he was discharged at Waldo, Florida, on May 20, 1865.

At the Battle of Gainesville, a horse was shot out from under him. He then mounted a riderless black horse of a fallen United States cavalryman. The saddle bags found on the horse contained silver articles (spoons and a cake container) which were subsequently handed down in the Gray family. Reportedly, Gray was involved in the capture and destruction of the U.S.S. COLUMBINE at Horse Landing on the St. Johns (north of Welaka). This took place on May 22, 1864, and the Confederate force was led by the famed Captain J. J. Dickison.[14] Gray had 17 of his men in that fray.

During the war, Hart engaged in carrying supplies for the Confederacy using his JAMES BURT and SILVER SPRING. Although Florida was officially blockaded by the federal navy, many cargoes got through the blockade. The usual route was from Nassau in the Bahamas to Mosquito Inlet (New Smyrna), Florida. Cargo was then carried by wagon to the upper St. Johns where it was transferred to small vessels such as the SILVER SPRING, JAMES BURT, and the Jacob Brock-owned HATTIE.

These steamers went to Welaka on the St. Johns and then on the Ocklawaha to Fort Brooke. Wagons took their cargoes to Waldo, on the recently completed Cedar Keys-Fernandina railroad. The goods would then go northward through Georgia to serve the southern states. The return cargo used to purchase the incoming goods was cotton, highly prized in Europe.[15]

Early in 1862, SILVER SPRING's captain, George Allen, received a letter from Major H. R. Teasdale, Confederate Quartermaster, instructing him to proceed to Volusia and take on board and transport to Orange Creek, two 8-inch Columbiads, fixtures, etc., said to be buried at or near Volusia. It was said there might be two other howitzers located about four miles from Volusia. These weapons were to be transported to Orange Creek, if they could be found.[16]

Later on in mid-December, 1864, the SILVER SPRING was chartered to the Confederacy at a rate of $200 per day. This duty lasted about 75 days and consisted of transporting "sugar and syrup for the Subsistence Department." Even though Lee had surrendered before the charter price was paid, Hart received the $11,000 due under the contract (65 working days during the period).[17] These are examples of the wartime career of SILVER SPRING.

Before buying the EMMA WHITE from Captain Gray, Hart had purchased the GENERAL SUMTER from the St. Marys Steamboat company on October 5, 1863. The latter was at Fort Brooke on the Ocklawaha River where she was in hiding from the Union forces. Hart paid $6,000 Confederate currency for her to S. G. Cabell, President of the Line.

Some 85 days later on December 29, he sold her back to a group from the company, H. L. Angier, Moses Cole, William Markham, I. W. Shackelford and S. G. Cabell, for $13,000. Hart also agreed "not to carry as freight on the SILVER SPRING more than 200 bales of cotton per annum from the mouth of the Ocklawaha River up the River St.

Johns during the present war or during the time the GENERAL SUMTER is running on that route."[18]

The close of the war saw the Grays in severe financial straits. During the war, Mrs. Gray with her two young girls and a three-week old son Harry, and with some family slaves, moved to Orange Springs for a year and thence to McMeekin where they engaged in farming, cotton being one of the crops. Captain Gray was a slave holder and much of his wealth before the war con- sisted of this form of "property".[19]

At the war's end, Captain Gray was virtually out of funds. His chief asset was $300 in gold, zealously guarded by his wife Eliza during the war. Most of the time she wore it around her waist in a money belt. Captain Gray used this money to build a barge to carry freight on the Ocklawaha. In the fall of 1865, the barge left for Silver Springs with a cargo. Three weeks were consumed in the round trip, and Captain Gray netted $500. Captain Gray then took two partners, ex-Confederate Major H. R. Teasdale and Robert R. Reid, and built the small META. The partnership was short lived.[20] Little is known of the META. An ancient woodcut shows a most decrepit vessel of that name, however, and she was probably the one that plied the Ocklawaha.

Hubbard L. Hart came out of the war fairly well off. He had only one active steamboat, the SILVER SPRING, but was rich in property. His pre-war vision of opening up the Ocklawaha region to trade was still with him, and he set out again to re-establish and extend his prior steam boat services. He also came out of the conflict with the title of Colonel, the official basis of which is uncertain. He had performed service for the Confederacy in 1862 by buying cavalry mounts in the Carolinas and Georgia. His known dealings with Confederate officers saw him not using the title. However, since everyone else at the time and for the rest of his life termed him 'Colonel', we shall do likewise.[21]

Before any major commercial travel could be resumed on the river, it had to be cleared of the many obstructions accumulated both naturally and through wartime neglect. Even the Confederates had realized its importance (from a military viewpoint) for they negotiated a $4,500 contract with Hart in February, 1865, to "remove the obstructions cut into the Ocklawaha River from Fort Brook to St. Johns River" and set a period of about four weeks for the work. Presumably, the SILVER SPRING performed the task.[22]

Hart also endeavored to be a timber baron, as in early 1866 he applied for "permission to cut cypress upon the Ocklawaha River and swamp (for) ten cents for each tree . . . (promising to give) bond for a faithful return of all trees cut . . . and prompt payment therefor."[23] This request was made to the Trustees of State of Florida's Internal Improvement Fund. His application was refused.[24]

Hart obviously realized he needed vessels, so in the years immediately after the war, he constructed a new fleet. In 1866, he built the GRIFFIN, #10835, 52.52 tons, at Palatka. Colonel Hart set up his shipyard at Hart's Point (across the St. Johns River from Palatka at a sharp bend). The Ocklawaha fleet to come would be regularly repaired there; a small marine railway was provided to haul vessels out of the water.

Ocklawaha River vessels were by no means pretty craft. Because of the unusual nature of the river, its tortuous bends, shallow water, snags and obstructions, the type of craft arrived at looked like a not-yet-completed houseboat erected on a rowboat shaped hull. Usually of two-deck construction, the lower one was devoted to freight and machinery and the upper to cabins for passengers. The GRIFFIN's pilot house was placed on the forward part of the cabin deck. It was not uncommon to build the steamboats in stages, each change and addition making a better vessel. In fact, only the last vessel of the Hart Line, the HIAWATHA, was built complete in its one and only form insofar as is known.

The most unusual feature of a typical Ocklawaha steamboat was the method of propulsion. A recessed stern paddlewheel was employed. About a fourth of the width of the vessel, it was almost completely enclosed in the center of the hull and superstructure. The wheel was turned by a pair of steam engines similar to those employed on a Western Rivers-type vessel. Doors opened at the rear of the vessel to let the churning water escape.

Rudders placed aft of the recessed wheel (and hull) gave these vessels good turning capability.

Usually, a single boiler and furnace supplied the steam necessary to feed the piston engines. The beam of the vessel was controlled by the narrow confines of the river and the length by its twists and turns. No vessel was wider than 23-1/2 feet and none longer than 89 feet.

Hart's second post-war vessel was the OCKLA-WAHA, #19109, 69.94 tons, built in 1867 or 1868. Much like the GRIFFIN, she was remodeled during her lifetime, the pilot house being moved to the top of the second or cabin deck. The OCKLAWA-HA and the GRIFFIN were the only Hart vessels equipped with parallel rows of windows for the second deck cabins.

The obstructions to navigation in the 130 miles of waterway needed to be cleared, and Hart set himself to that task. In October, 1867, in response to Hart's application, the Board of Trustees of the Internal Improvement Fund covenanted with Hart to "remove the obstructions to the navigation of the Ocklawaha River (in return for) donations of (state-owned) land to enable him to do so."[25] The Board granted "the Swamp and Overflowed and Internal Improvement Lands, embraced in the odd-numbered sections, lying within ten miles of the Ocklawaha River, and the Lakes supplying said River . . . For every expenditure made by . . . Hart in removing said obstructions . . . Hart shall receive the amount thereof in lands at the present prices, provided that said expenditures do not exceed the amount of twenty thousand dollars."[26]

By mid-January of 1868, Hart reported expenditures of $5,495, and lands to that value were conveyed.[27] By mid-March, further expenditures of $3,638 were experienced, and lands to that value were transferred.[28] Hart showed excellent progress in his work as by the end of August he reported expenditures of just over $8,000.[29] The project was finished by November of 1868 when Hart reported expenditures of $5,063, bringing the total above the $20,000 agreed upon.[30]

To do this work and carry on some semblance of a passenger business, Hart had the GRIFFIN, OCK-LAWAHA and SILVER SPRING. The GRIFFIN was the work horse of the fleet in the clearing work. To assist, a derrick-equipped scow, the PIONEER, with Joseph H. Smith as master, was provided. Cap-

tain David A. Dunham was master of the GRIFFIN during this time. Later he would be found on the OCKLAWAHA and other Hart Line vessels, but he spent most of his career in charge of Hart's shipyard and repair facilities at Hart's Point.[31]

Captain Joseph H. Smith was a veteran master of St. Johns River steamboats and had a varied career in a variety of vessels. He would be associated with Hart off and on during his lifetime.

Masses of floating and decaying vegetation and thousands of feet of dead or water-logged trees had to be removed from the water as did submerged logs, snags and other hazards to navigation. Leaning trees hung out over the river from the banks, and limbs always threatened passengers on the vessels. It is reported that in a 15-mile stretch of the river, some 300 trees were removed from the banks and 172 logs from the bottom.[32] Floating islands of vegetation were a perplexing problem which Dunham solved by sawing them into pieces and moving them onto flooded lowlands where they rooted after being staked out.[33]

In 1868 or 1869, Hart built the very crude PAN-SOFFKEE. She was of 32.87 tons and her official number was 20349. She was hopefully named in honor of Hart's latest attempt at expansion, an attempt to reach the Gulf of Mexico via the Withla-coochee River!

A dozen land miles separate Lake Harris from Lake Panasoffkee, which empties into the Withla-coochee. If a canal between the two lakes could be furnished by dredging, imagine the commercial possibilities. Hart attacked on two fronts, the state and the federal, the latter by getting a bill introduced in Congress to grant public lands in return for canal construction. The terms of the bill introduced in Congress were such as to make the project infeasible.[34]

Hart instead settled for state permission to improve navigation to the lakes area, to wit, "Hart (was) permitted to make, cut or dig a canal from Lake Eustis to Lake Dora, a canal from . . . Lake Dora to Lake Apopka and a canal from Lake Griffin to Lake Harris, to make . . . canals between Lake Griffin and the shoals above Silver Spring run, in the Ocklawaha River and to dredge such shoals on said River in the State of Florida. Each of said canals or cuts to be made navigable (for) barges and steamboats of not less than 20 feet beam. Hart to be granted lands as (before)."[35] Nothing came of the attempt, however.

By the time the PANSOFFKEE was completed, SILVER SPRING was no more. Whether she was dismantled and her machinery placed in another vessel or had met her fate on a lonely stretch of the river is unknown. Hart still had three vessels, however, as the 1860s drew to a close. It was only a few years after the war, but tourists were finding the state, and the Ocklawaha River and Silver Springs.

Since the river was quite well cleared by now, Hart was much the richer in lands, and regular schedules of his vessels were being published. In 1869, a steamboat left Palatka every Thursday for Lake Griffin. A steamer (or steamers) ran twice a week from Palatka to Silver Springs. (It is not clear whether the vessel to Lake Griffin was counted in the above, but it is probable.) The running time from Palatka to Silver Springs was 40 hours and the fare but $5.00.[36,37] The schedule was also dependent upon receiving tourist passengers at Palatka from Charleston and Savannah steamboats. Usually the heavy-duty, sea-going side-wheelers, DICTATOR and CITY POINT, delivered these visitors during the week, and the Ocklawaha-bound craft met them accordingly.

In 1871, the schedule was about the same. The GRIFFIN was the Silver Springs boat, leaving Palatka on Thursdays and Silver Springs on Saturdays for the return trip. The OCKLAWAHA was the "through" boat to Okahumpka. Leaving Palatka on Sundays, Okahumpka on Wednesday and Silver Springs on Thursday, she barely arrived back in Palatka in time to get ready for her next trip.

PANSOFFKEE was placed on a new route on the St. Johns River, Palatka to Crescent Lake (then called Dunn's Lake), which was reached through Dunn's Creek, a tributary of the St. Johns. This was a once-a-week trip, and Hart's Captain A. L. Rice was the PANSOFFKEE's master.[38]

Hart's three steamers were not without competition. Getting back to Captain Henry Gray, we find that in 1870 he sold part of his property for $400 and borrowed some additional money to build his MARION, which came out the following year. The MARION, if possible, was more crude and less pretentious than any of Hart's vessels. Her official number was 90399, and she was 78 feet long by 18 feet wide, and of 67.43 tons. The eminent Sidney Lanier was aboard her in 1875 to view the "Springs" and ensconced on a piece of the deck furniture, with his feet on the rail, watched the passing primeval panorama. At night the deck hands rendered plantation melodies against the swamp-like surroundings as the boat crept along.[39]

Brinton (in 1869) described his second river trip including listing a few landings and points of interest. For example, "Davenport's Bluff (12 miles from the mouth on the right, it had a few houses); the Narrows was eight miles long, Blue Springs on the right bank was 17 miles above the Narrows. Fort Brooke was 26 miles further. Orange Spring did not have accommodations for travelers."[40]

Above Silver Springs, Brinton noted, "no change in the monotony of the cypress swamp occurs for about sixteen miles . . . the cypress disappears, and a savannah covered with dense saw grass stretches on either side for one or two miles from the river. . . . After passing through these savannas some miles the boat enters Lake Griffin . . . then to Lake Eustis, (six miles beyond Lake Griffin).

"Beyond Lake Eustis a deep channel a mile and a half long leads to Lake Harris. . . . The Oklawaha enters it at its southwestern extremity. . . . Next (is) Leesburg. About five miles above Lake Harris is Lake Dunham, the head of navigation of the Oklawaha. A settlement on this lake bearing the name Oklawaha is the terminus."[41]

The Ocklawaha steamboats occasionally made trips from Jacksonville to Silver Springs, a route that added five to seven hours to the schedule time (from Palatka). However, as the vessels that regularly plied between Jacksonville and Palatka appeared in bigger and better versions, the practice gradually subsided, and the Ocklawaha navigation headquarters remained at Palatka. Over the years, however, many Ocklawaha vessels sporadically made the long trip as trade or special occasions might demand.

In 1873, Colonel Hart constructed his OKA-HUMKEE at his East Palatka (Hart's Point) shipyard. Destined to be an extremely long-lived vessel, she was to undergo considerable change during her long tenure, all of which served to make her an improved, more useful vessel. Her name was consistently misused from the mid-1880s on. At that time the name boards on the craft were changed to read 'OKEEHUMKEE', a name she held until toward the end of her days. (A surviving photo of her even shows her named 'OKAHUMKEE.') Her name was also listed as OKAHUMKA, OKAHUMPKA, OKEEHUMPKEE and even OKEEHUMKEE 2nd (the latter in Hart literature only). Always, however, she remained the same vessel.[42]

She was reportedly named after a legendary Indian chief who lived around the area of the headwaters of the Ocklawaha lakes. A town in that area is also named Okahumpka.

The next Hart Line vessel was OSCEOLA, built at Palatka in 1874. The OSCEOLA, of course, was named after the great Seminole Indian leader who had lived near the Ocklawaha River area of Florida many years before. Like her companion OKAHUM-KEE, OSCEOLA was to undergo many changes over the years. She was #19433 and was 83.2 feet by 20.4 feet and her hold depth was 5.2. Gross tonnage was 86.54 tons. Steam for the vessel was provided by a simple locomotive-type boiler that was 16 feet long and 2 feet, 10 inches in diameter. Allowable steam pressure was 100 psi. She had two diminutive non-condensing steam engines, each with an 8-1/2 inch diameter cylinder and a 2 foot, 6 inch piston stroke that drove her recessed stern wheel.[43] The two vessels in effect replaced the GRIFFIN and OCKLAWAHA, although it would be a few years before that duo was abandoned.

Travel literature of the time was rife with accounts of journeys on the Ocklawaha vessels.

Harpers Magazine described such a trip in its January, 1876, issue. "Our comical little steamer, not unlike a dwarfed, two-storied canal-boat, had started out boldly from the Pilatka dock that morning with its full quota of twenty passengers on board, six feet of shelf having been carefully engaged in advance by letter or telegram for each person.

"It was now night and the steamer had stopped. . . . Suddenly flared out a red light from above, and, as if by magic, the weeds grew red. . . . Birds cried from their near nests and flew past our faces; the steamer started on, carrying the magic with her. Pitch-pine fires had been started in braziers on top of the boat to light the way, and, tended by a negro boy, they burned brilliantly all night, sending a red glow over the dark waters ahead, showing the sudden turns, the narrow passes, the bent trees and a lonely little landing, where we left a barrel for a solemn old mule which came down and inspected us as the steamer ran her bow on shore - the ordinary way of landing on the Oklawaha. . . .

"At this moment we heard in the distance a far sound in answer to our doleful cry. 'The other steamer.' said the Baptist brethren on the roof, who passed down bulletins gathered from the pilot. 'They have to warn each other in order to find a broad place to pass in.'

"We soon saw a gleam up the river high above the trees, glancing from side to side in the air, for the boat was still some distance off, and the course of the stream tortuous. In the meantime our little craft had crowded herself ignominiously close to the shore that one side was tilted up like a buggy turning out for another on a narrow mountain road. She clawed the bank so desperately that involuntarily we drew our very skirts back. . . . At length . . . a sudden glare shot over the river in front of us. Round a curve came the other steamer, her pitchpine fires blazing high on top and the little decks below crowded with passengers. . . . Cheers exchanged.

"In the mean time the two boats were passing each other gingerly, scraping the shores on each side, the respective cooks exchanging a few whispering confidences from their little windows as their black faces were carried slowly past each other only a few inches apart. Then we watched the glare glide on down the river.

"That night we met the incoming steamer. And now it was her turn to claw the bank, while we sailed majestically on down the stream, our fires proudly burning on top."[44]

Competition to Hart was already present in Gray's MARION, but in 1875, the TUSKAWILLA, #145082, was built at Leesburg. One could almost describe her as being 'pretty', and in the matter of details she was superior to her Hart competitors. In contrast to Hart's vessels, she had an 'artistic' polygonal pilot house. Her railings were supported on turned, carved balusters. The passenger cabin front had a large, 'curved-at-the-top', leaded-glass window that graced her. Her lettering was more ornate than that of her competitors also. Her owners at that period are not known.

In 1878, she ran from Jacksonville to Palatka, Silver Springs, Leesburg and "Okahumkee" on a once-a-week basis. Captain A. N. Edwards was her master, and her departure was from S. G. Searing's wharf, foot of Pine Street, Jacksonville, on Thursday at 8 a.m.[45]

One of the owners of the TUSKAWILLA, as early as 1879 and continuing on into the early 1880s, was Dr. S. J. Bouknight of Palatka, and later, Jacksonville. In November, 1881, she was advertised as making the trip from Jacksonville to Silver Springs and Leesburg once a week, leaving at 8:30 a.m. (day unknown).[46]

In the mid-1870s, Hart's little PANSOFFKEE came to the end of her days. Always rather small, even for her time, she was listed as being 'broken up' in 1875.[47]

In 1876 and 1877, Hart shifted his OCKLAWAHA to run between Fernandina and Palatka. She had had a major rebuilding, and her pilot house was raised atop her refurbished cabins. Twin ladders replaced the single one to the second deck. Fernandina had long been a center for waterborne traffic and was a good transfer point. Because of its deeper harbor depths, vessels from New York called on a regular basis. The OCKLAWAHA carried some of her passengers to new homes in Florida and for a time provided a "missing link" service between Fernandina and points south.[48]

By the year 1878, both the GRIFFIN and the OCKLAWAHA were gone (GRIFFIN in 1874 and OCKLAWAHA in 1877). Again, the official disposition is "abandoned." Both had managed to serve over a tough decade of demanding service.

Another competitor of Hart's in the 1870s was the FORESTER, an 1871 vessel built at Norfolk, Virginia. She came to the Ocklawaha in 1878. She was probably a recessed sternwheeler (judging from the only photo found showing her at a Palatka dock with the LOLLIE BOY and OCKLAWAHA). Her number was 9966 and she was of 69.82 tons. She was in the area only a relatively short time (1878 to perhaps 1882) and was registered at both Jacksonville and Palatka. For part of this period she was operated by S. J. Bouknight. She is officially listed as 'lost' in 1882 and may have terminated her career in a wreck.[49]

Concerning the TUSKAWILLA and the FORESTER, in 1881 and 1882 (if not before), they were part of Dr. S. J. Bouknight's line of Ocklawaha River steamers. In 1881, the TUSKAWILLA was advertised to leave Palatka at 9:30 a.m. for Silver Springs on Mondays, Wednesdays and Fridays. The FORESTER left for Leesburg and 'Okeehumkee' on Thursday evening after the arrival of the Charleston steamer.[50]

By the end of the decade of the 1870s, Hart was in a position to buy out his long-time competitor, Captain Henry A. Gray. In fact, he not only did so, but retained Captain Gray in his employment for many years. In early November, 1880, Henry Gray sold his MARION to Colonel Hart for $2,000, a small sum indeed. Captain Gray initially remained on as the MARION's skipper, although he did command other craft for Hart, especially the ASTATULA, until the end of his working days.

The MARION was extensively rebuilt around this time (the low purchase price might indicate after the sale) and reappeared as a substantial craft much like the OKAHUMKEE of the 1880s.

The OSCEOLA was the host to General Ulysses S. Grant in January of 1880, when he, too, succumbed to the lure of the Ocklawaha trip. Starting his venture at Welaka on January 11, he ascended the river to Silver Springs and tarried a spell at Ocala. At the time he was "sounding the waters" on public attitudes concerning his seeking a third presidential term. He was complimentary of his Ocklawaha trip and of his conveyance.

A national weekly described the conclusion of the river trip., "When the boat reached Harrison's Landing there was a crowd of men and women, white and colored, who had come many miles. . . . The Mayor came on board and after meeting General Grant said, 'Fellow-citizens of Marion County, I have the honor to introduce to you General GRANT, the most distinguished living American.' The crowd gave one of those shrill Southern cheers, so unlike the deep, sonorous ring of the Northern hurrah. As many people as could find room on the boat came aboard, and the steamer proceeded on to the spring a mile away, where there was another throng that cheered. The curiosities of the spring inspected, General GRANT and some members of the party were driven in carriages to Ocala, the county seat of Marion."[51]

In 1882, an additional steamer in service was the WAUNITA (of which more later). She was advertised as having been added to Bouknight's service and a daily schedule provided, still leaving Palatka at 9:30 a.m. for Silver Springs. The WAUNITA's companion was the TUSKAWILLA, and the round trip took 35 hours. At Silver Springs, the WAUNITA connected with the FORESTER for Leesburg on Tuesday, Thursday and Saturday.

Bouknight's office was in Palatka on the north side of Lemon Street.[52] He and his brother operated a store featuring groceries, fine liquors and 'segars.'[53] Dr. Bouknight was a competitor of Hart, of course, but the extent of his operations and their durability and duration are pretty much unknown.

Bouknight's WAUNITA, #80874, was completed in Jacksonville early in 1882. She was a trim-looking craft, rather dainty, in fact. She was 77 feet long, 22 feet wide and had a 3-foot depth of hold. She was of 63 gross and 49.77 net tons.[54] Uniquely, she had twin stacks instead of the usual one. She was initially registered at Palatka for two years. She possessed a recessed sternwheel, and from this feature, it seems obvious she was destined for the Ocklawaha River.

The WAUNITA's construction progress was noted by the Florida Union. In mid-January, it was indicated, "Dr. Bouknight's new steamer, the WAUNITA, is now at the ship-yard. She will be ready for service in a very short while and will be the largest and finest passenger steamer on the Ocklawaha River."[55] Twelve days later, the paper noted that the WAUNITA "is rapidly nearing completion."

The existing photos of her show that her cabin deck had side windows that were curved or arched at the top. She had a polygonal pilot house, double ladders from her lower to upper cabin deck and a single ladder to her pilot house. Like the TUSKAWILLA, she had a curved-top, front cabin deck window. Her wood railings were supported by carved balusters similar to those of TUSKAWILLA. In length and other characteristics she was similar enough to TUSKAWILLA to have been designed and built by the same person.

In November, 1881, the Hart Line advertised four vessels as being in service. The OKEEHUMKEE, Captain A. L. Rice, ran to Eustis once a week, leaving Palatka on Thursday; ASTATULA left Palatka on Saturdays at 6 p.m. The vessels returned on Tuesday and Fridays. The OSCEOLA, Captain Dunham, and the MARION, Captain Gray, made trips to Silver Springs, probably three trips per week each.[56]

Another vessel, owned by Colonel Hart and Captain Joe Smith, the FLORA, was on local service from Jacksonville to Green Cove Springs on the St. Johns, and intermediate landings, leaving Clark's wharf in Jacksonville at 2:30 p.m. In the morning, she left Green Cove Springs at 7 a.m. John Clark, a prominent Jacksonville merchant, was the FLORA's agent.[57]

The FLORA had been built in Brooklyn, New York, in 1874 and enrolled in 1879 at Jacksonville. She was #120139 and was 75 feet by 16.8 feet by 4.9 feet. Her gross tonnage was 86.48. She had one deck, no masts and had a plain head and a round stern.[58]

Hart's winter schedule was adjusted in January, 1882. The OKEEHUMKEE, Captain A. L. Rice, and the OSCEOLA, Captain A. N. Edwards, left Palatka six days a week at 9 a.m. for Silver Springs. At the Springs, the ASTATULA, Captain Gray, connected twice a week for Leesburg, Lakes Griffin, Eustis, Harris and "Okeehumkee."[59]

On February 4, 1882, the Florida Union indicated that the WAUNITA was now running on the

Ocklawaha. "The saloon is finished in hard woods and the furniture is the finest that could be found at Cleaveland and Sons store in this city. The side board alone (cost) several hundred dollars." Evidently she had started her service about the first of February. Also, in that month, perhaps in response to the WAUNITA, Hart adjusted his schedules and had the ASTATULA leaving on Mondays at 6 p.m. for the long trip to Leesburg and return.[60] As an indication of the freight carried, the OKEEHUMKEE made a mid-December arrival in Jacksonville with 480 boxes of oranges and 34 bales of cotton.[61]

George M. Barbour described a January, 1880, trip on the OSCEOLA. He indicated, "The steamers . . . are each an aquatic curiosity. Built especially for the route, they are altogether unique; there are (none) anywhere like them. . . . They have an appearance of having been placed in service just before completion. Constructed with two decks - quite low between - a snug little square-shaped wheel-house high up forward, and a tiny lobby deck aft, with the row of three or four little state-rooms ranged between, they are unexcelled for the accommodations which they offer in the scanty space at command; and are a much more comfortable and serviceable craft than their appearance would indicate.

"Upon the roof of the wheel-house of our special steamer was a large iron box where a bonfire of pitch-pine knots lighted up the scenery (at) night. A huge sternwheel furnished the propelling power. The cabin was quite neat, but a perfect little doll's house in size and furnishing . . . but it was big enough to afford accommodation for all, there being but four or five passengers other than our party."[62]

Negro pilots were regularly employed by the Hart Line. These pilots had authority over the deckhands and wheelmen. Hart printed rules for his vessels which directed that "neither the pilot nor the wheelman should make a 'bend alone, and that at night, anywhere, without the Captain's aid, not a minute should elapse without two men in the pilot house.'"[63]

The practice of employing blacks was in sharp contrast to that employed elsewhere such as on the Mississippi. Many St. Johns river vessels also utilized black pilots.

The decade of the 1880s was a good one for the Hart Line despite the Bouknight competition. The FORESTER went out of existence in late 1882 or early 1883. The TUSKAWILLA was to last until 1887, but news of her after 1882 is scarce. The WAUNITA, through unknown circumstances, was involved in a wreck on the St. Johns. Captain Joe Smith bought her as a sunken wreck in mid 1884, had her salvaged and towed to Palatka. There, with his partner, Colonel Hart, he hoped to have the needed repairs performed at Hart's yard. However, the shipyard was unavailable and Smith, using the FLORA, towed her to Jacksonville and had the repairs accomplished there.[64]

The mid-1880s were the height of steamboat activity on the St. Johns. In a few years railroad competition would severely curtail traffic on that river and also contribute to the demise on the Ocklawaha, and the steamboat trade would dwindle away.

In 1881, Colonel Hart built his last vessel, the ASTATULA. Similar in appearance to the OSCEOLA, she was 80.6 by 20.6 by 3.6. Her official number was #105964 and she was of 55.96 gross tons. Slightly smaller than OKAHUMKEE and OSCEOLA, her most distinctive feature was the narrow 'promenade' deck area around the cabin. She received the customary twin stairs to the cabin deck in later years, and the promenade deck was removed and the cabin widened to the full width of the steamboat. Over ten years later she finally received her second cabin deck.[65]

The ASTATULA commenced her service on the river in 1881 but was shifted to another route for the 1884-1885 tourist season a few years later.

Going back a few months to March of 1883, we find that Hart, in partnership with Joe Smith, had started a steamboat line from Lake Monroe to Lake Poinsett on the upper St. Johns. The normal heads of navigation for regular size vessels on the St. Johns were Enterprise and Sanford, both on Lake Monroe. As the Indian River area of Brevard County opened up to settlement, the travel to it was fostered by using shallow draft steamboats on the upper St. Johns. Rockledge on the Indian River was only three miles away from Lake Poinsett on the St. Johns via a short overland portage.

In March of 1883, Hart diverted his MARION from the Ocklawaha to the upper St. Johns route. Captain Joe Smith was her master, and the MARION's schedule called for her to leave Enterprise every Monday and Friday (connecting with the DeBary Line steamboats from Jacksonville) for Rockledge. A year later the ASTATULA joined the line, and at times when water conditions were right, runs were even made to Lake Winder on the St. Johns.[66]

With the advent of Smith's WAUNITA in early 1885, the Rockledge service was designated as "Hart and Smith's Rockledge Line for Indian River." The MARION went back to Ocklawaha service, and the WAUNITA and the ASTATULA maintained the upper St. Johns service.

The ASTATULA and the WAUNITA provided a joint service through the 1885-86 season, but business was bad due to the advent of railroads. In April, 1886, the ASTATULA went back to Palatka and did not return. She became the spare boat on the Ocklawaha for the 1886-87 tourist season. The WAUNITA may have stayed another year on the run but then gradually drifted into Hart's Ocklawaha fleet, perhaps as a spare vessel.

An English traveler described a trip on the Rockledge Line on the WAUNITA. "This little vessel, which navigates the ... upper St. Johns River, where a larger craft could not pass, is very comfortably fitted up, small as it is. We cast appreciative glances around the prettily decorated little saloon, with its sofas and rocking chairs; we inspected the tiny sleeping-rooms, with their clean white berths, and presently carried out two easychairs on to the little strip of deck forward of the saloon, and sat down to enjoy the landscape in peace and comfort, and in the society of our fellow passengers, who also, one and all - fortunately the 'all' was not a crowd, as the slip of deck was narrow! - brought their chairs and camp stools outside.

"One of our fellow-passengers takes such delight in all these things that his gratitude overflows toward the authorities through whom he obtains the privilege of this day's enjoyment.

"His enthusiasm finds vent in the grateful exclamation - 'Now I call it real good of the Captain and company to give us this beautiful trip for five dollars.'

"This gentlemen's appreciation extends to the certainly excellent meals which are served to us in the neat little saloon. His encomiums embrace the tender venison steak, the cutlets, the eggs, the fish, the hot biscuits.

"In the morning we find ourselves at our landing place, Lake Poinsett, but we do not land until we have enjoyed a good breakfast on board the WAUNITA."[67]

Some idea of how little food cost in the Hart Line's heyday and why fares could be kept so low is furnished by a perusal of a grocery list of April, 1886, for the OSCEOLA and OKAHUMKEE. Sugar was 8-1/2 cents per pound; butter, 23.3; lard, 10; rice, 7; cheese, 18; four quarts of apples went for 25 cents, flour was 4 cents a pound; hominy, 2.5; coffee, 30; 11 pounds of ham cost $1.54. A five percent discount was subtracted from the above.'[68]

For a time after the demise of the Bouknight competition, opposition to the Hart Line was sporadic and relatively nonproductive. A Captain Howard, presumably of the Howard family of Grahamville, constructed a vessel at Norwalk, Florida. She turned out to be the ALLIGATOR of 1888. Her engine was installed at Palatka, and she was originally equipped with a screw propeller, later changed to a recessed sternwheel.

The ALLIGATOR, #106613, was 57 by 18.7 by 3.5. She was originally of 24.71 gross tons. In 1890, her length was increased to 71 feet and in 1897 to 81.4 feet. Her tonnage ultimately went to 69 tons.[69] Although around for several years, she seems not to have been placed on any substantial commercial service or regular route.

For several years, however, Dr. Clarence B. Moore of Philadelphia, an amateur archaeologist, used the ALLIGATOR to pursue his hobby of excavating all the Indian shell mounds he could find in the Ocklawaha and St. Johns area. The vessel proved to be an excellent floating repository for his collection.

The MARION was the next vessel to go.

In 1887, she was the spare vessel for Hart; in 1888, she may have run without documentation.

In 1890, she and the OKEEHUMKEE made several 'end of the season' runs to Jacksonville. That is the last we hear of the MARION, and she disappears from view.[70]

Times were changing, railroads were penetrating the area, and increasingly the Hart Line business was concentrating on the lure of Silver Springs as a tourist mecca. Obviously, adjustments had to be made to accommodate changing tourist patterns.

Until the early 1890s the Hart craft ran pretty much on an annual basis, although admittedly on a reduced schedule in the off-season summer months. December to April became the dominant tourist months, and the boats laid up for the rest of the year and were repaired at Palatka. While the advent of the 1890s would see another competitor emerge, the end of the decade of the 1880s signalled also the end of the Hart Line's best days. The 1890s would be times of challenge and decreasing opportunities and diminishing financial returns.

The next competing vessel was the EUREKA of 1890. Built at Silver Springs, she was #136160 and was 69.6 by 16 by 4 and of 79.62 gross tons. Mitchell indicates sardonically that she was 'easily among the five homeliest steamboats ever constructed.' Her machinery deck was open most of the way to the rear of her boiler and then covered with vertical-laid planking around the stern, leaving an opening for the access door of the recessed paddlewheel. She had a small cabin and a diminutive funnel aft the pilot house. She is usually pictured at Silver Springs and she may have been just a day boat used for local excursions. She was owned by Captain J. Ed. Lucas, a Palatka boat owner who was also involved in a ferry service there. In 1878, Thomas Dardis and he operated a boat livery business there (steam yacht, sail and rowboats).[71,72]

The challenge of the 1890s to Colonel Hart occurred with the advent of a new and extremely competitive vessel, the METAMORA. She was finished in 1893 at Palatka, and her builder was Captain Lucas. The METAMORA was certainly the finest craft built to this time for passenger service on the Ocklawaha. She featured a passenger promenade area on all four sides. Interior companionways were substituted for the Hart steamers' exposed outside ladders. An elaborate polygonal pilot house was provided, and the funnel was generally an improvement over those found on the Hart vessels. Moreover, the METAMORA was built 'complete' whereas all the contemporaneous Hart vessels had evolved over the years.[73]

Colonel Hart had kept a weather eye out on Lucas' activity, and he countered by extensively rebuilding the OKEEHUMKEE. Never very aesthetic, she emerged larger than her competitor and with two complete tiers of cabins. She was also equipped with a new boiler 17.8 feet long, 4 feet in diameter with a working pressure of 115 psi and a maximum allowable pressure of 160 psi. Her engines were slightly larger than those of the OSCEOLA, and each had a 10-1/4 inch diameter cylinder with a 2 foot, 6 inch piston stroke.[74]

Thanks to the Historic American Merchant Marine Survey (HAMMS) of the 1930s, conducted by the Smithsonian as a WPA-type project, we are able to ascertain what materials were used in the building and rebuilding of the OKEEHUMKEE. Yellow pine was used for the keel and stern. Durable cypress was employed for planking, beams, floors, decks, frames and ceilings. Oak was used for the bitts and stem, and the vessel was fastened with galvanized spikes and bolts. Her recessed paddlewheel was 10-1/2 feet in diameter and 3-1/2 feet wide. Her draft was only 1 foot, 10 inches. Her overall length was 84 feet, 2 inches, and her length at the water line was 82 feet, 2 inches.

The METAMORA was #92487 and was 87 by 21.5 by 3.4. Her gross tonnage was 165.07, and she was by far the largest vessel on the river based on the tonnage measurement. She was lettered 'METAMORA' in big bold letters on her upper cabin, and in even larger letters, 'Lucas New Line', was emblazoned on her lower cabin.

Colonel Hart countered in 1894 by enlarging the ASTATULA and striking the OSCEOLA from his active list. It should be noted that the WAUNITA had been stricken from the official list after 1892. The ASTATULA had an upper cabin constructed atop her single cabin deck which was less than the full width of the supporting cabin.

Schedule-wise, in 1895, the OKEEHUMKEE, Captain Harrison, and the ASTATULA, Captain

Howard, left Palatka at 1:30 p.m., six days each week. Lucas countered with his METAMORA by sending her out an hour earlier on Monday, Wednesday and Friday.[75]

The METAMORA competed heavily against Hart, benefiting from advertising and rate cutting. Meanwhile, Hart's ability to counter was adversely affected by several misfortunes in 1895. The freeze of that year, the first that far south in many years, wiped out Hart's extensive orange groves, the freights of oranges were severely lessened, and the cold weather saw to it that the tide of visitors trickled to an ebb. Finally faced with the potential loss of his line, Hart made a deal with Captain Lucas, namely, a consolidation of the two lines. This was accomplished in early December. The event took place only a few days before Colonel Hart's untimely and accidental death on December 12, 1895, when he was fatally injured alighting from a trolley car in Atlanta, Georgia.[76]

Earlier in the year, on April 3, Captain Henry Gray, then in his 69th year, departed this life. His death, coupled with the later death of Hart, brought an end to the pioneer era on the river.[77]

Hart's place in the Ocklawaha Navigation Company (the official name of the Lucas and Hart interests) was assumed by his New England brother-in-law, R. H. Thompson of Boston. Hart had married Miss Thompson in 1884 and was wealthy enough to be able to spend the next ten summers in Boston where he was known as the "Orange King." During the past few years of Hart's financial distress, Thompson had made funds available to help overcome the straitened circumstances under which the Hart Line had labored. And, of course, the consolidation had at least stabilized conditions, even if it was only a temporary expedient. Mitchell credits Thompson with saving the line and extending its life another quarter of a century, a great achievement under the circumstances that were to ensue. However, consolidated service or not, the Ocklawaha trade had seen its best days.[78]

Business seemed to average out to less than half the capacity of the vessels making up the service. Surviving Hart records analyzed by Mitchell show an average of 20 passengers for each upbound trip

in the three months of the January to April season of 1896 and 15 passengers per downbound trip.

During this same period, the passengers ate the best the country could afford. Dinner in April, 1896, cost a whole 50¢! Some of the viands were rib roast, steak, stew meat, sausage, pork chops, ham, turkey, chicken and mullet. Other staples were eggs, potatoes, bacon, brown sugar, macaroni, mince meat, crackers, lemons, cabbages, cheese, tapioca, cakes, syrup, apples, and that southern standard, grits. The meat prices of the day are astounding: rib roast, 15 cents per pound; steak, 18; stew meat, 8; sausage, 12-1/2; pork chops and ham, 12-1/2; turkeys, $1.00; chicken, 30; four mullet at 25 cents. Eggs were 15 cents a dozen.[79]

Starting with the 1897-98 tourist season, the Lucas interests and those of Thompson drifted apart and the consolidation ceased to exist. Each went on its own, the METAMORA under the Lucas banner and OKEEHUMKEE and ASTATULA under Thompson auspices. Another characteristic of the journey from Palatka to Silver Springs was that a majority of the travel was now one way in nature. The other (return) leg of the journey was made by another transportation mode, railroad.

It is rather absurd to think of Ocklawaha steamboats racing on that narrow stream. Certainly there were few stretches where one vessel could pass another. However, in 1903, F. R. Swift set forth his witnessing of such a race on the river.

". . . as we rounded Hell Gate Island into the upper river the Lucas Line boat loomed ahead, with the opposition boat only twenty feet behind. It was once again the rivalry of the Mississippi boats in the old Mark Twain days. The two had been nip and tuck all night long. They were now hugging each other for a spurt in the fairly open water of the last mile run. Then there would be fun. The leading boat now had the right of way and puffed along like a fat king with the asthma. The trailer could do nothing but trail, for she couldn't pass the leader without pushing her into the woods. The passengers on the decks were howling and clasping each other's hands with excitement."[80]

Thompson also owned and ran several Palatka-based boats shortly after the turn of the century.

They were used in local service and served the St. Johns-oriented properties in the area. The vessels were the propellers EDITH and FEARLESS and the sternwheeler GAZELLE. EDITH, #136062, was 50 by 13.1 by 3.6 and of 15 gross tons. She was built in Harlem, New York, in 1883 and registered in Jacksonville in 1890 and was last registered in 1902.

The FEARLESS was constructed at Palatka in 1897. She was #121045 and 50 by 15.3 by 3.1 and of 24.05 gross tons. The GAZELLE, #85994, was 56 by 18.5 by 3 and of 52.69 tons. She was built at Georgetown in 1888 and owned by the Hart Line from 1895 until 1903 when she was last registered.

A smaller vessel, the IDA MAY, was also owned by Thompson. Captain Dunham owned a small propeller, the PUTNAM, which served as a local water taxi and ferry vessel, perhaps also catering to excursionists. The PUTNAM, #105276, was built in Palatka in 1883. She was 66.7 by 12.7 by 3.2 and of 17.03 gross tons. She was last registered in 1900.

The year 1903 saw a competitor to the Hart Line emerge in the form of the WILLIAM HOWARD. Built in Palatka, she was 85 by 21 and of 97 tons. The Howard family of Grahamville on the Ocklawaha River constructed and operated the vessel. The WILLIAM HOWARD operated a more casual schedule and also catered to the freight business on the river.

Accidents were rare on the river and fatalities even fewer, but in 1903, both occurred. The METAMORA was the ill-fated vessel. At about 3 a.m. on the 19th of March, the METAMORA, while nearing the junction of the Ocklawaha with the St. Johns, rounded a sharp bend and heeled hard to the left, crashing into trees while doing so. Bouncing back from the impact, the METAMORA settled in 20 feet of water. Two negro boys, Walter Watson and Rufus King, sleeping in the fore port of the hull, drowned.

The impact of the trees fortunately had awakened most of the passengers and sleeping crew. The engineer, captain, and crew assembled the 28 now-aroused passengers on the METAMORA's cabin roof. By daylight a batch of rowboats, added to the boats of the METAMORA, had arrived at the scene

and transported all to Welaka. The Hart Line's FEARLESS then took them to Palatka.

The METAMORA's captain had left the pilot house for a few winks and was not "on duty." Supposedly, due to a large deckload of wood fuel, she was badly trimmed, and there was some possibility of water already being in the hold. A snag was also suspected, and there was some suspicion of "pilot error." At any rate, the post mortems were inconclusive as to pinpointing the exact cause.

The METAMORA was raised and was probably taken to either Welaka or Palatka where she was photographed in a sunken condition. It is not known whether she was ever fully repaired and ever ran again, but it is doubtful. However, she was registered until 1908.

The Hart line celebrated the demise of their chief competitor by constructing an entirely new vessel, their "Queen of the Line." This was the HIAWATHA of 1904. Still using Indian names, this time a more popular and well-known name was chosen. HIAWATHA, #200729, was 89 by 23.5 by 4.6 and of 129 gross tons.

The HIAWATHA carried 80 first class cabin and 10 deck passengers and had 10 staterooms on her saloon deck and 18 on the upper one. She had two stacks placed abreast of each other. She was equipped with an internal rear staircase, although the forward area still had outside stairs. She had two water tube boilers 5 feet, 4 inches long by 20 inches in diameter that operated at 170 psi. Her twin condensing engines had 11-inch diameter cylinders with 3-1/2 foot piston strokes and had been built by the Buckeye Foundry and Machine Shops of Keokuk, Iowa. Her pilot house was styled like that of the METAMORA.

The Hart Line was now under the management of R. W. Thompson who had taken over from his brother R. H. Thompson. Another Thompson, A. S., was the General Passenger Agent. With the advent of the HIAWATHA, the fleet consisted of three vessels, the others being OKEEHUMKEE and ASTATULA. The FEARLESS had been sold but still ran out of Palatka.[81]

The HIAWATHA ran a schedule similar to that of METAMORA, leaving Palatka at 12:45 p.m. and arriving at Silver Springs before noon of the following day. Allowing her passengers a few hours at the Springs, she then left at 2 p.m. and arrived back in Palatka in the early morning of the following day. Only a January through April schedule was maintained.

In the summer of 1905, due to the death of his father, the operation of the WILLIAM HOWARD was taken over by J. Hatten Howard, II, until 1910 when he sold out. The new owners then had extra staterooms built on the vessel's upper deck, and she was renamed TOURIST. The venture failed financially, and the vessel was tied up at Palatka where she sank. Captain Howard, after looking at her for a year, bought her cheap, raised her, and then towed her to Jacksonville. He had her stern cut off just forward of the recessed sternwheel, lengthened her to 125 feet and had a regular-type sternwheel installed. Howard ran her between Jacksonville and Daytona Beach until the water shoaled up and he quit. In Howard's words, "she made a beautiful sternwheeler."[82]

The late 1910s saw the Hart Line making its rounds during the winter season, still a tourist-passenger business. Ever increasing reams of publicity were devoted to the virtues of the service and travel agents were quick to exploit the novel trip.

In 1912, the ASTATULA was taken out of service and tied up at the river edge near Hart's Point. She gradually lost much of her superstructure and had almost disappeared completely by the 1930s. She was "gone" by the time the HAMMS vessel survey was made in the mid-1930s.

In 1909, the ownership of Silver Springs passed to C. (Ed) Carmichael. He promptly set out upon an aggressive campaign of promotion and luring northern tourists. One of his first steps was devoted to providing a better fleet of glass-bottomed vessels at the Springs. He also decided to start a daylight service of vessels on the Ocklawaha River, based, of course, at Silver Springs. A railroad connection made in 1903 had brought visitors from the north directly to the Springs and many wanted a trip on the river.

In 1912, Carmichael launched an internal-combustion powered craft, the CITY OF OCALA. She was #209614, 37.6' long, 13.4' wide and had a 3.5' hold. She was of only 13 gross tons. She had two decks and had a pleasant yacht-like appearance. Based at Silver Springs, she made trips to Palatka every other day. The fare was $5.50 one way and $10.00 for a round trip. Her first trip started in the 1913 season, and it was obvious that the new competition boded ill for the Hart Line. In 1914, the CITY OF OCALA was lengthened to 44.9 feet. Her indicated horsepower at the time was a diminutive 40. A few years later the two-decked SILVER SPRINGS was put into service. SILVER SPRINGS was #212898 and her dimensions were 43.4 by 14.0 by 4.3 and she was of 31 gross tons. She was built in 1915 at Silver Springs. Her horsepower was also 40.

In 1915, the Hart Line countered with their iron steamboat BILLOW. She was #212705 and 56.8 by 14 by 4.3 and of 30 gross tons. She had been built in 1887 at Wilmington, Delaware. Her schedule indicated that she left Palatka on Tuesday, Thursday and Saturday at 7 a.m. Her fare was $5.75 one way and $10.50 for a round trip. The trip was made completely in daylight.

The Hart publicity was quick to point out the safety virtues of its twin-propeller, iron-hulled vessel. "The steam power is from the small tubes of the non-explosive safety Taylor and Almy Water Tube Boilers, in marked contrast with the well-known dangers attending other methods of propulsion. All Hart Line steamboats have large observation decks, large and comfortable steam-heated, glass-sided cabins (steam heat being a necessary adjunct) and toilet rooms for ladies and gentlemen, all protected from cold winds."[83] Apparently the BILLOW only ran one year on this route.

Carmichael's Silver Springs Transportation Company countered, "They have two decks, are swift, safe, and provided with every convenience. Modeled on graceful lines, driven by powerful, high-powered gasoline engines, they are the ideal boat for a pleasure boat on an inland waterway. Every safety regulation required by the United States inspectors has been provided."[84] By this time a third vessel had been added, the WEKIWA. WEKIWA, #207988, was 46.4 by 11.2 by 3.3 and of 19 gross tons. She was built in 1910 at Palatka and had a 24-horsepower engine.

A comparison of the crew requirements for the Hart Line and its competition indicates the disparity of costs experienced.

WEKIWA, CITY OF OCALA and SILVER SPRINGS, 3 crew members each. OKAHUMKEE (18 crew) and HIAWATHA (15 crew). In 1915 the traditional iron basket of pine wood knots on the HIAWATHA was replaced by an electric searchlight. Armed with this, she returned to the fray and served through several seasons including that of 1918-19, along with the OKAHUMKEE (described in company publicity from 1917 to 1919 as the OKAHUMKEE 2nd).

Carmichael and his three vessels won out after the 1919 season as, before the 1920 season could be started, the Hart Line decided to throw in the towel and published this notice:

"Ocklawaha Steamboat Co., Palatka, Fla., Dec. 9, 1919. The scarcity of skilled shipyard help, due to the previous absorption by shipyards and industries far away, obliges this company to postpone its winter time schedule, till further notice by mail to all principal ticket agents! R. W. Thompson, Gen. Mgr."[85]

By 1921, the OKAHUMKEE and HIAWATHA had been dropped from official registry and were listed as being "abandoned," and the BILLOW as "sold Cuban". The Silver Springs Transportation Company continued until sometime beyond the mid-1920s.

As the 1920s dawned, the OKAHUMKEE and HIAWATHA entered a new era, that of being onlookers. The HIAWATHA was hauled out of the water on to the marine railway where she had been built, and the OKAHUMKEE was moored at the nearby river bank where she settled to the bottom and gradually rotted away.

In the mid-1930s, workers for the WPA project, the Historic American Merchant Marine Survey, (HAMMS), surveyed and photographed the two vessels and drew plans of them. The OKAHUMKEE was razed soon after the survey was made, but the HIAWATHA continued to be on view on shore until 1979. At that time she was only a bundle of rotting wood but still maintained the looks of a steamboat. Much of the nearby property was sold as part of a real estate development, and the vessel was demolished as a safety hazard.

The P. W. Thompsons, successors to the Hart Line owners, memorialized the Hart Line by placing many of the two vessels' mattresses, mirrors and bedspreads in their "Hart's Point Tourist Court." This property was located on U.S. Highway 17 just south of the bridge over the St. Johns River. The window curtains had red hearts placed on them, as a token of the bygone "Hart Line."[86] Nowadays, even these vestiges of the Ocklawaha have disappeared. The tourist court property was acquired for a wider St. Johns River-U.S. 17 bridge approach.

Another river service, the Mills Steamboat Line, was in business from 1908 until 1919. It was established by Everett Lee Mills in the fall of 1908, chiefly for the purpose of hauling freight from the Moss Bluff area to Delk's Bluff. There the WILLIAM HOWARD would receive it for shipment to Palatka or Silver Springs. Mr. John Sewell and Oliver Edwards had acquired a barge which had been used as a ferry at the Grahamville crossing and used it as a pole barge. Tiring of the laborious upstream trip, they hired Mr. Everett Lee Mills to install a gasoline engine in it. Sewell and Edwards, not being familiar with gasoline engines, sold the powered barge to Mills, who placed a bow on it. Because of a loud popping noise made when the engine operated at low speeds, the vessel was termed the SHARP SHOOTER.

After two years of this operation, Mills constructed a new vessel, also named SHARP SHOOTER. She was just under 65 feet in length and had a four-cycle engine. Launched in April, 1910, she was active in carrying turpentine, then coming into being as an industry, and other products such as oranges, hides and stock for stores between Palatka and Silver Springs.

The SHARP SHOOTER connected with the Seaboard Airline Railway at Silver Springs and Vertree's and Company at Palatka. Stops along the way were made at Delk's Bluff, Grahamville, Conner, Durisoe's, Gore's Landing, Sunday Bluff, Eureka, Iola, Payne's Landing, Orange Springs, Jordan's, Ft. Brooke, Riverside, The Narrows, Piney Point, Brobery, Mouth of the Ocklawlaha, Norwalk, Welaka, Buffalo Bluff, Dunn's Creek, San Mateo, Browning's, and Palatka.

An occasional stop along the way was at 'Starling's Log'. This was an old log at the river's edge where a Mr. Starling lived. He would leave a list of things he needed from Palatka, and Mills would pick up the list and do Starling's shopping for him. Starling, as well as others along the river, would have several dozen of eggs to sell for them, and Mills obliged in this regard also.

The SHARP SHOOTER continued this service until sometime in 1917 when she was replaced by another vessel, designed and built by Captain Mills. This vessel was named the HEL-KAT, a combination of the names of his two young daughters, Helen and Kate. This vessel, also under 65 feet in length, had its pilot house raised, which made for more room for freight. Vessel-manning rules at the time were more favorable for vessels under 65 feet in length, so that was a consideration in designing a ship.

When World War I came along, business along the river slowed, and help was hard to get, so in 1919, Captain Mills retired from the river. The SHARP SHOOTER was left at its mooring to decay, and the HEL-KAT was sold.

A negro pilot on the WILLIAM HOWARD was Forest "Rail" Wright, so nicknamed because of his slenderness. He finished his river career on the SHARP SHOOTER as one of the pilots. Other Negro pilots were Henry Counts and Emanuel Myers, and Captain Mills' granddaughter believes they were the best steamboat pilots ever to navigate the crooked Ocklawaha. Another pilot and mate on the SHARP SHOOTER was Jack Wellhoner (1913 to 1917), son-in-law of Mills.

The pilothouse wheel of the HIAWATHA and several other artifacts are on view at the Bronson House, the headquarters of the Putnam County Historical Society in Palatka. A representative model and photographic materials on exhibit there serve to remind one of the old river days.

Fine models of the OKEEHUMKEE and HIAWATHA have been built by Ralph Lossing of Melrose, Florida. The Jacksonville Maritime Museum exhibits the OKEEHUMKEE and plans to exhibit the HIAWATHA in due course.

OCKLAWAHA RIVER RIVERBOATS
"PADDLE-WHEEL - INBOARD"

Barges powered by "POLES" were the first commercial vessels on the Ocklawaha River. They were powered by groups of men (often slaves) who used the poles to push the barges along the river.

Riverboats on the Ocklawaha River started around 1850 and continued until 1920 when gasoline-powered boats and the railroads began to take over the hauling of passengers and freight from Palatka to Ocala and returning.

The Riverboats were powered by "wood burning boilers". The wood was bought by the cord, a stack of wood 4 feet wide, 4 feet high, and 8 feet long. Some of the boats would use as many as 18 cords of wood for a round-trip from Palatka to Silver Springs. The cost per cord was around $2.00.

The "fare" for passage for a round-trip ticket from Palatka to Silver Springs was about $10.00. This included berth and meals.

The trip from Palatka to Silver Springs would vary from one to two days to as much as five days, depending upon the boat.

The boats leaving Palatka would bring various supplies to the "settlers" along the river and to Silver Springs, and they would return to Palatka carrying oranges, cotton, eggs, turpentine, chickens, and other things they could buy along the river.

The distance from Palatka to the mouth of the Ocklawaha River is 25.5 miles. The distance from the mouth of the Ocklawaha River on the St. Johns River to Silver Springs was 109 miles, with 999 bends in the river.

A "fire box," an iron box about 4 foot square, using pine wood was used to light up the river for running at night.

The Riverboats would average about 18 feet wide and 85 feet long with a draft of about 4 feet. The length, width, and draft were limited due to the depth of the water, the narrow width, and sharp bends.

The "PADDLE-WHEEL INBOARD" term means the paddle-wheel was positioned inside the boat at the stern for protection from the tree limbs.

- Michael C. Mason

Riverboats steaming on the Ocklawaha and Silver Rivers.

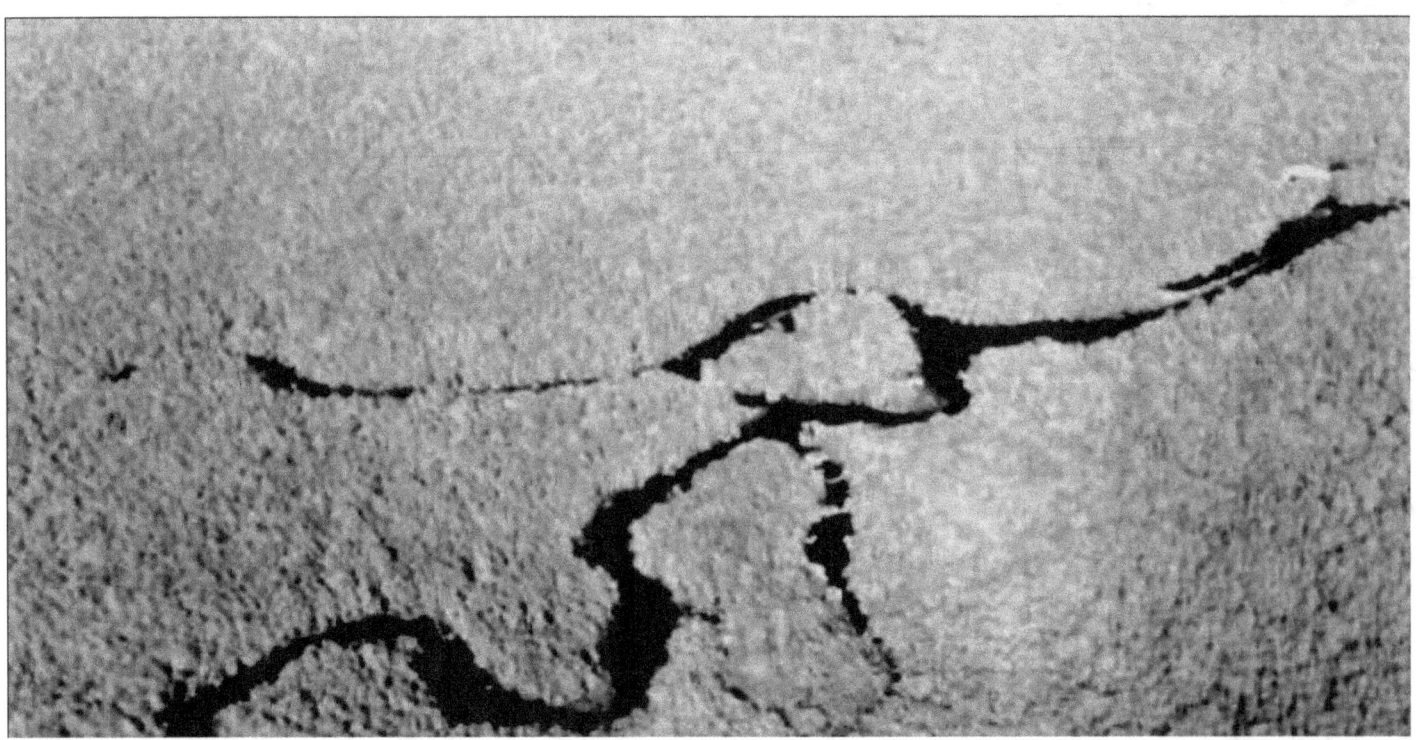

These two images show how the Ocklawaha River got its Native American name as "dark crooked water".

A Trip Over Crooked Water

Kirk Munroe, the Victorian Age chronicler of Florida fact and fiction, produced "A Trip Over Crooked Water", which appeared in *Harper's Weekly*, Volume 27, 1883. Descriptions of travel on the Ocklawaha abound and Munroe's description is typical and perhaps less exaggerated than many others. The account follows:

"No visitor to Florida who has any regard for his own peace of mind can leave the State without having made the trip up the Ocklawaha River, at least to Silver Spring. He may have explored every other river in the State from its source to its mouth, but if he has neglected this one river, his friends who have sailed its 'crooked waters' will insist upon it that he has failed to see the brief object of interest, and really knows nothing of Florida. In itself the Ocklawaha is no more remarkable than a dozen other rivers in the State, nor is Silver Spring more wonderful than several others which are hardly ever visited, but they come within the radius of the mainline of winter travel, while the others do not. However much people may enthuse over the delights of the wilderness, and announce their love of 'roughing it,' the popular routes of travel are always those upon which are the most comfortable sleeping accommodations and the best set tables. In Florida the great highway of travel is the St. John's River, up which boats run three hundred miles south from Jacksonville. At Tocoi, fifty miles up the river, the traveller branches off to the eastward, and takes the little fifteen-mile railroad to St. Augustine; and at Palatka, twenty miles further up, on the opposite side of the river, he halts, if he is bound up the Ocklawaha.

"A night's stay in Palatka is imperative, because all boats reach there in the afternoon, and all the Ocklawaha boats leave there in the mornings. So at Palatka—a place in which there is little to see and less to do—the traveller spends an afternoon and night as best he may, and by nine o'clock next morning is ready and anxious to break the monotony of existence there by a trip up the Ocklawaha or any other river that promises interest and variety.

"The Ocklawaha River boats, five in number, are *sui generis*, built expressly for the navigation of this particular stream, and all alike in general features. They are short, narrow, flat-bottomed, built without guards, low, and compact. Their chimneys rise but little above the roof of the pilot house, in front of which, or on the lower deck forward, are the seats which the passengers occupy all day, and far into the night, while viewing the novel scenes constantly presented during the journey. As compared with the rude, awkward craft of a few years ago, these boats are models of comfort, and are admirably fitted for the service they perform. They are all of the stern-wheel or "wheelbarrow" pattern, each wheel being so inclosed as to be protected from contact with overhanging trees or branches. Most of them bear Indian names, such as OSCEOLA, OKAHUMKEE, ASTATULA, or TUSKANILLA (sic); and often during the winter the rush of travel is so great that three of them filled with passengers leave Palatka at the same time.

"Starting at nine o'clock in the morning, the boat, with her merry company—for Ocklawaha River travellers are proverbially jolly fellows— steams for three hours up the St. John's, to Welaka, on the left bank, opposite which the 'crooked water,' which is the meaning of the Indian word 'Ocklawaha,' debouches into the larger stream, and here the trip really begins. The moment the broad St. John's is left behind, the character of the scenery changes. Entering the narrow, wonderfully tortuous channel, winding through vast cypress swamps, and bordered by a dense' growth of magnificent trees hung with moss and interlaced with a maze of vines and creepers, is like plunging from an open clearing into a dark forest. Palms and other strange forms of semi-tropic vegetation fascinate the eye, and new and curious specimens of animal life present objects of never-failing interest. The alligator, which to Northerners is the greatest curiosity in Florida, and which is now rarely seen from the decks of the St. John's River boats, here becomes common, and at length fails to arouse any great amount of interest. So clear is the water that frequently the 'gator,' startled from his siesta among the 'bonnets' or rushes on the bank, can be seen making his way far beneath the surface to a more secure retreat. Shooting from the deck of the steamer, which was allowed during the earlier days of Ocklawaha navigation, became such a nuisance, and so threatened the destruction of some of the leading attractions of the river, that it is now strictly prohibited, much to the disgust of those fledgling sportsmen who look upon every species of undomesticated bird or beast as their legitimate target, and to the satisfaction of all sensible travellers.

"Although the alligator is the star and leading attraction in this grand spectacle, he is ably supported by a select feathered troupe, which are to be seen at their best in these watery fastnesses. Most beautiful of these is the great snowy heron, which, with his companion the great blue heron, is such a treasure to the curiosity dealers, and works up so effectively into a fire-screen. At every bend, perched upon some dead limb, is seen the comical water-turkey or snake-bird, stretching his long neck, and ducking his head in a ridiculous state of indecision as to whether he shall fly or not, and finally solving the problem by dropping like a shot into the river, and disappearing beneath its surface. His cousin the cormorant shares his indecision, and affords almost as much amusement as the water-turkey by his frantic and erratic efforts to escape the approaching steamer. The speckled limpkin attracts attention at once by the peculiarly discordant cry, not unlike the laugh of a hyena, with which he makes his presence known, and which may be heard echoing through the dismal swamps at all hours of the day and night. A limpkin's egg is about the size of a hen's egg, and very good to eat. Beside these are the ibis and egret, the crane, curlew, and many others, curious in form and habit.

"The various landings along the river afford but little idea of the country beyond, as most of them are merely shedlike warehouses, built upon shaky little wharves, and connected with the mainland by roads of corduroy laid through the swamps. They bear such names as Sunday Bluff, Limpkin Bluff, Forty-foot Bluff, Iola, Gores, Eureka, and Duerisosa (sic), and the few cadaverous-looking natives, whose straight, lank hair and dirty homespun suits form prominent features at each landing, do not convey in their forms or countenances any re-assuring impressions as to the healthfulness of the adjacent country. But who cares for malaria or chills and fevers when on a trip up the Ocklawaha? They can't be contracted in one day, and none of the gay party of tourists have got to live there; so, with a word of pity for the unfortunates who must make this their home from one year's end to the other, the subject is dropped, and attention is again directed to the river.

"A steady subject of inquiry is, 'When shall we pass the down boats?' And when about sunset their whistles are heard and answered, all hands crowd to the best positions for seeing and exchanging greetings with the returning tourists as they pass. If the place of meeting is very narrow, as is generally the case, the upward-bound boats hug the bank closely, and wait for the others to pass. As the boat on which our artist was making his first trip up the river thus drew to one side to give the others room, a comical accident occurred that came very near being serious. Beside our artist sat an enthusiastic old gentleman whose jolly face and bald head were surmounted by a tall and very shiny silk hat. With him were his two pretty daughters, and the three were in a state of great excitement over the meeting of the down boat, on which they expected to see friends. The old gentleman, having attached his (hat) to his gold-headed cane, was waving it high above the others, when suddenly there was a jar of the boat, a crash overhead, and from a tall cypress, into which the up boat had run while hugging the bank too closely, a dead limb came tumbling. It struck fairly on the top of the shiny silk hat, drove it down over the beaming face, and scattered twigs and splinters over the rest of the passengers. In the confusion which followed, the down boat passed unheeded. Nobody was hurt, and it was as good as a play to see those two pretty girls strive to release their father from the envelopment of that now disreputable looking silk tie. The lining caught on his rather prominent nose, and every attempt to lift the hat elicited a howl of pain from the old gentleman, and much vigorous language. At length a release was effected by the aid of the ready penknife of our artist, and soon afterward, with a swollen nose, and disguised by an old slouch felt hat borrowed from the captain, the respectable father of the pretty girls presented the typical aspect of a venerable rake, just emerged from a rough-and-tumble melee.

"The greatest enjoyment of a trip up the Ocklawaha comes after the sun has set, and the scenery is enveloped in the blackness of a dark night. A burning brand is thrust among the resinous light-wood knots that fill an iron fire-pan on top of the pilot house. A burst of flame springs forth, and discloses by its yellow glare a scene so weird and uncanny as to baffle description. The black water shimmering in the fire-light, the gaunt tree trunks rearing themselves into an upper vagueness, from which depends, straight and motionless, the cere-ment-like hangings of gray moss, the dark lagoons penetrating the swamps, and bordered by fantasti-cally horrible forms, the hurried flight of startled night birds, all combine to form a picture that will remain forever indelibly impressed upon the minds of those who view it. The passengers involuntarily gather closer together, and talk in more subdued tones, as they gaze upon the rapid unfolding of the wonderful panorama, which fascinates them as by a spell. Suddenly a few chords are struck from a banjo on the lower deck, and a dozen rough but melodious voices break out in some old plantation melody abounding in minors and longdrawn re-frains, and in perfect harmony with the hour and surroundings. One of these songs was so similar to those sung by the Arab boatmen on the Nile that for the moment the writer felt himself to be sitting on the little deck of a dahabeeyah, floating down with the smooth current of the majestic Egyptian river. The first few lines were:

'All night long,
Jesa, Jesa,
On my knees,
Jesa, Jesa,
Begging God,
Jesa, Jesa,
To gib me ease,
Jesa, Jesa.'

"The refrain 'Jesa, Jesa,' running through the song in a bass monotone was identical with the 'Allah, Allah,' or 'Moosa, Moosa,' of the Arabs, and lent the peculiar rhythmical drone that forms so prominent a feature of Oriental melodies.

"A few of the passengers remain on deck until nearly midnight to witness the passage of the 'gate of the Ocklawaha,' which is simply the passing of the steamer through a channel so narrow that there is barely room for it, and bounded on either side by an immense cypress-tree; but the majority retire early, in order to be up in the morning in time to see the 'Run.'

"Soon after daylight the boat leaves the river, and, turning sharply to the right, enters the 'Run,' a stream so clear that it is like a body of crystal glass confined by wooded banks. For nine miles the steamer makes her way against the swift current of the 'Run.' Its bottom is of white sand, from which spring long feathery grasses and other beautiful forms of marine vegetation, that wave in the trans-parent waters as though tossed by currents of air. At the end of the nine miles the boat glides over the bosom of Silver Spring, and runs up to a little wharf on its further shore. A cushioned row-boat awaits the tourist who would still further explore the won-drous beauties of the spring, and in a moment after entering it he experiences all the sensations of an aeronaut. His boat has become an airship, and it's floating in thinnest ether, high above the world, down upon which he gazes. So still is the water, and so wonderfully distinct the shallows, that a photo-graph taken of some object upon the bank of the spring is equally accurate whether inverted or held upright.

"Silver Spring is wonderful, and as well worth seeing as though it were the only one of its kind in the State, and it well repays the two hours allotted to its inspection. At the end of this time the trav-eller either returns to his boat, which is prepared for the return trip to Palatka, or takes the Southern Railway, and arrives in a few hours, instead of will be the case with the boat.

"Some idea of the crookedness of the Ocklawaha may be gained by comparing the distance travelled by the steamers between Palatka and Okahum-kee, the head of navigation, which is 275 miles, with that of an air-line, which would be but eighty. Very truly does the name 'crooked water' apply to this mysterious river; but in this very crookedness lies its chief charm, which is that of constant antic-ipation."

KIRK MUNROE

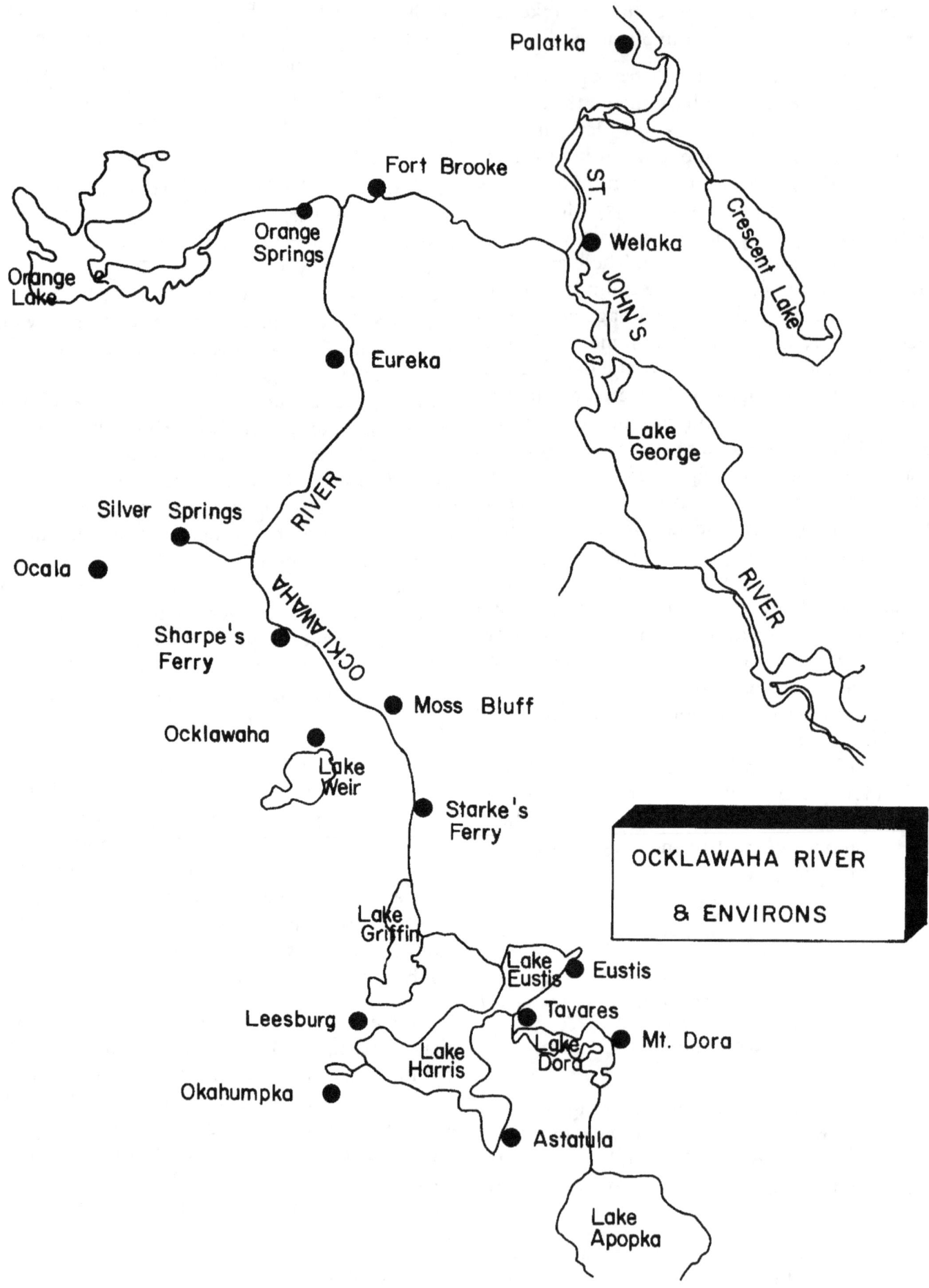

Palatka

Fort Brooke

Orange Springs

ST. JOHN'S

Welaka

Crescent Lake

Orange Lake

Eureka

Lake George

RIVER

Silver Springs

Ocala

RIVER

OCKLAWAHA

Sharpe's Ferry

Moss Bluff

Ocklawaha

Lake Weir

Starke's Ferry

Lake Griffin

Lake Eustis

Eustis

OCKLAWAHA RIVER

& ENVIRONS

Leesburg

Tavares

Lake Dora

Mt. Dora

Lake Harris

Okahumpka

Astatula

Lake Apopka

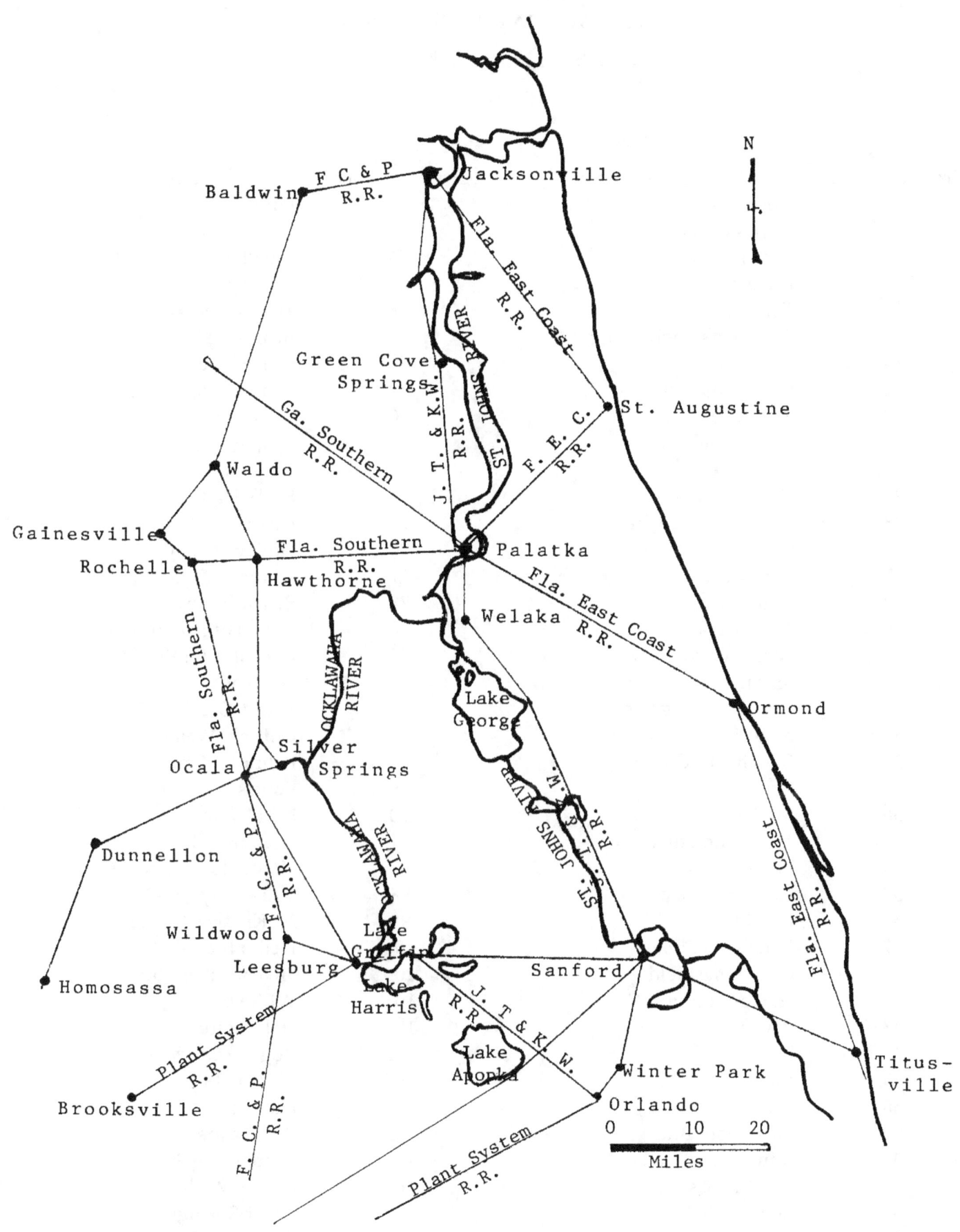

Ocklawaha and St. Johns River Railroads
1880's

OCKLAWAHA RIVER LANDINGS
St. Johns River to Silver Springs
Circa 1890

Miles (from entrance)	Landing Name	Miles (from entrance)	Landing Name
3	Double SS	59	Eureka
4	Boyd's Creek	62	Cypress Gate
6	Bear Island	65	Pine Island
7	Davenport	67	Sunday Bluff
8	Toney's Hole	68	Twin Cypress
12	Poorman's Labor (Pinner's)	69	Bear Tree
14	Narrows	69	Star Island
14	Freeborn's Cut	69	Sunday Run
15	Riverside	70	Fern Tree
18	Deep Creek	71	Hogan's
19	Jack Gates	72	Pin Hook
20	Turkey Creek	73	Hell's Half Acre
23	Blue (or) Salt Spring	74	Park's
25	Cedar	75	Dodger Island
27	Jam Log	77	Gore's
28	Agnew's	78	Brush Heap
29	Turkey Foot	80	Straits of Darrin Kenels
31	Fort Brooke	81	Osceola's Old Field
32	Jordan's	83	Durisoe's
33	Orange Spring Shoal	85	Stuart Creek
34	Needle's Eye	86	Chitta's Avenue
35	Enoch and Collins	88	Palmetto Grove
36	Gray's Cut	89	Long's
36	McBride's	90	Mill View
33	Twin Palmettos	91	Grahamville
34	Long Reach	95	Howard's
35	Harper's Ferry	98	Shime Taylor
36	Big Eddy	99	McKroski's Old Field
37	Matchett's Shoals	100	Delk's Bluff
39	Crowningshield	100	Silver Spring Run
42	Hart's Secession Camp	101	White Oak
43	Payne's	101	Helvington's
47	Douglas	102	Rogers' Grove
49	Iola	104	Marshall's
50	Well's	106	Pasteur's
52	Forty Foot Bluff	107	Robinson's
54	Rough and Ready	108	Turpentine Still
54	Cut Chief's Sign	109	Jacob's Wells
55	Log Landing	110	Silver Springs
57	Eureka Cutoff		

OCKLAWAHA RIVER LANDINGS

Palatka to Silver Springs

As Listed on Hart and Lucas Combined Line Schedule Card, 1901

Miles	Landing Name	Miles	Landing Name
—	Hart's Grove	75	Iola
2 1/4	Rolleston	77	Well's
5	San Mateo	78	Forty Foot Bluff
7	Dunn's Creek	79	Rough and Ready Cut
8 1/4	Murphy Island	81	Ed Moore Cut-off
9 1/2	Buffalo Bluff	85	Log Landing
18	Satsuma	86	Eureka Cut-off
19	Nashua	87	Eureka
20	Root's Wharf	87 1/2	Cypress Gate
22	Three Sisters	94	Sandy Bluff
25	Welaka	95	Twin Cypress
25 1/2	Ocklawaha Mouth	97	Bear Tree
29	Boyd's Creek	98	Star Island
31	Bear Island	100	Hogan's
32	Davenport	100 1/2	Pin Hook
37	Poor Man's Labor (Pinner's)	101	Hell's Half Acre
39	Narrows	102	Park's
39 1/2	Freeborn's Cut	102 1/2	Dodger
40	Riverside	103	Gore's
43	Deep Creek	103 1/2	Brush Heap
44	Jack Gates	104	Straits of Dardin Kennels
45	Turkey Creek	105	Osceola's Old Field
48	Blue (or) Salt Spring	108	Duriso's
50	Cedar	113	Roger's
52	Tuskawilla Cut	114	Stuart Creek
54	Sims	115	Chitty's Avenue
54 1/2	Honey Bee	116	Palmetto Grove
58	Fort Brooke	117	Long's
58 1/2	Jordan's	118	Grahamville
59	Orange Creek	120	Howard's
60	Needle's Eye	122	McKroski's Old Field
61	Gray's Cut	125	Delk's Bluff
61 1/2	McBride's	126	Silver Springs Run
62	McBride's Cut	127	White Oak
63 1/2	Indian Bluff	129	Helvington's
64 1/2	Twin Palmettos	130	Rogers Grove
64	Long Reach	131	Marshall's
67	Big Eddy	132	Pasteur's
68	Matchett's Shoals	134	Robinson's
69	Crowningshield	134 1/4	Turpentine Still
69 1/2	Hart's Secession Camp	134 1/2	Jacob's Wells
73	Payne's	135	Silver Springs

OCKLAWAHA RIVER LANDINGS

Silver Springs to Palatka

From Silver Springs Daylight Route Brochure, 1919 Season

Miles	Landing Name	Miles	Landing Name
1/4	Jacob's Wells	48	Eureka
3/4	Turpentine Still	49	Eureka Cutoff
1	Robinson's	57	Forty Foot Bluff
2	Fossil Bone Yard	60	Iola Indian's Home Site
3	Pasteur's	62	Payne's Battle
3	Carmichael	66	Crowningshield
4	Marshall's Ground	67	Matchett's Shoals
5	Roger's Grove	68	Big Eddy
6	Sistrunk	70	Twin Palmettos
8	White Oak	71	Indian Bluff
9	Ocklawaha Junction	73	McBride's Cut
10	Delk's Bluff	73	McBride's
16	Grahamville	74	Gray's Cut
17	Randall's Orange Grove	75	Needle's Eye
17	Conner	76	Orange Creek (Orange Spring Landing)
18	Long's		
19	Palmetto Grove	76	Jordan's
20	Chitty's Avenue	77	Fort Brooke
21	Stuart Creek	78	Mound Builder's Home Site
21	Duriso's	81	Sims
31	Osceola's Last Battle Field	83	Tuskawilla Cut
31	Shell and Sand Mound	85	Cedar
32	Gore's	87	Blue (or) Salt Spring
32	Dodger Island	90	Turkey Creek
33	Park's	95	Riverside
33	Mound Builders' Village of Seven Mounds	96	Narrows
		98	Pinner's
34	Hell's Half Acre	103	Davenport
34	Pin Hook	104	Bear Island
35	Hogan's	109	Mouth of Ocklawaha
37	Star Island	110	Welaka
38	Bear Tree	117	Satsuma
40	Twin Cypress	130	San Mateo
41	Sunday Bluff	135	Palatka
47	Cypress Gate		

PROMINENT FEATURES AND DISTANCES
AND LANDINGS ON THE OCKLAWAHA RIVER*

Miles	Landing Name	Miles	Landing Name
3.1	Turpentine Creek	43.7	Stuart's Creek Lower
4.3	Bear Creek Point	45.4	Osceola's Last Battlefield
6.9	Davenport Point	45.7	Drisco Landing Rogers Cut
8.2	Poor Man's Labor	46.5	Lower End
10.1	East River Side	46.7	Upper End
10.3	Riverside	47.4	Stuart's Creek Upper
12.2	Deep Creek	47.9	Caldwell Landing
15.2	Dutchman's Reach	48.6	Long's Landing
15.8	Cedar Landing	48.8	Shingle Mill
16.4	Hemmenway's Landing	49.2	Conner
18.2	Agnews Landing	49.6	Turkey Creek Landing
18.8	Turkey Creek	50.1	Grahamville Ferry
20.4	Fort Brooke Landing	51.2	Howards Landing
21.0	Jordan's Landing	52.2	Delks Bluff
21.3	Orange Spring Creek	52.3	Golbys Landing and Site
21.3	Orange Spring Landing		of Daytona Bridge
22.2	Palmetto Heights	52.6	Silver Springs Run
23.0	McBride's Landing	53.6	Juliet Creek
24.8	Wells Landing	55.0	Sharpe's Ferry Bridge
25.3	Indian Bluff	58.2	Heather Island Landing
26.5	Tobacco Patch Ferry	58.6	Heather Island Ferry
27.0	Raines Landing	58.6	Old River End
27.6	Douglas Landing	59.6	Kyle-Young Canal
27.9	Iola Landing	63.9	Young's Landing
29.8	Forty Foot Bluff Landing	64.5	Fort's Landing
33.7	Eureka Bridge Sunday Bluff	66.2	Moss Bluff Bridge
37.1	Lower End	66.3	Moss Bluff Lock and Dam
37 2	Upper End	73.7	Starke's Ferry Road
40 8	Palmetto Landing	77.5	Emeralda Dock
41.5	Wood Landing	78.8	Lake Griffin
42.2	Gore Landing	86.5	Leesburg (via canal)

*Measured from the Mouth of the Ocklawaha (at the St. Johns River).

*These Distances and Points on the River are as Set Forth by the U.S. Corps of Engineers, Measured in *Direct Miles* and as Recorded in 1935.

OCKLAWAHA RIVER VESSELS

Official Number	Vessel Name	Year Built	Place Built	Tonnage	Length	Width	Depth
	OCKLAWAHA (barge)	1854	Jacksonville	—	—	—	—
	FAWN	1855	Jacksonville	—	52	10	—
	GENERAL SUMTER	1859	Palatka	41.95	—	—	—
	EMMA WHITE	circa 1860	—	—	—	—	—
	JAMES BURT	circa 1860	—	—	—	—	—
23066	SILVER SPRING	1860s	Palatka	73.95	—	—	—
10835	GRIFFIN	1866	Palatka	52.52	60±	18-20	—
19109	OCKLAWAHA	1867 or 68	Palatka	69.94	60-70	18±	—
20349	PANSOFFKEE	1868 or 69	Palatka	32.87	50-60	18+	—
9966	FORESTER	1871	Norfolk, Va.	69.82	—	—	—
90399	MARION	1871	Palatka	67.43	78	18	8
19409	OKAHUMKEE[1]	1873	Palatka	65.14	84.4	21.4	8.3
19433	OSCEOLA	1874	Palatka	86.54	83.2	20.4	5.2
145082	TUSKAWILLA	1875	Leesburg	76.48	71	21	8
105964	ASTATULA	1881	Palatka	55.96	80.6	20.6	3.6
80874	WAUNITA	1882	Jacksonville	63	77	22	3
212705	BILLOW	1887	Wilmington, Del.	30	56.8	14	4.3
136160	EUREKA	1890	Silver Springs	76.92	69.6	16	4
92487	METAMORA	1893	Palatka	76.92	69.6	16	4
106613	ALLIGATOR	1893	Palatka and/or Norwalk	24.71	57	18.7	3.5
				—	71	—	—
				69	81.94	—	—
81854	WILLIAM HOWARD[2]	1903	Palatka	97	85	21	—
				84	108.3	20.4	4
200729	HIAWATHA	1904	Palatka	129	89	23.5	4.6
207998	WEKIWA	1910	Palatka	19	46.4	11.2	3.3
209614	CITY OF OCALA	1912	Silver Springs	13	37.6	13.4	3.5
					44.9		
212898	SILVER SPRINGS	1915	Silver Springs	31	43.4	14	4.3

[1]Also officially named OKEEHUMEE, called OKAHUMKA, OKAHUMPKA, OKEEHUMPKEE, OKEEHUMKEE 2nd.

[2]Renamed TOURIST for a brief spell.

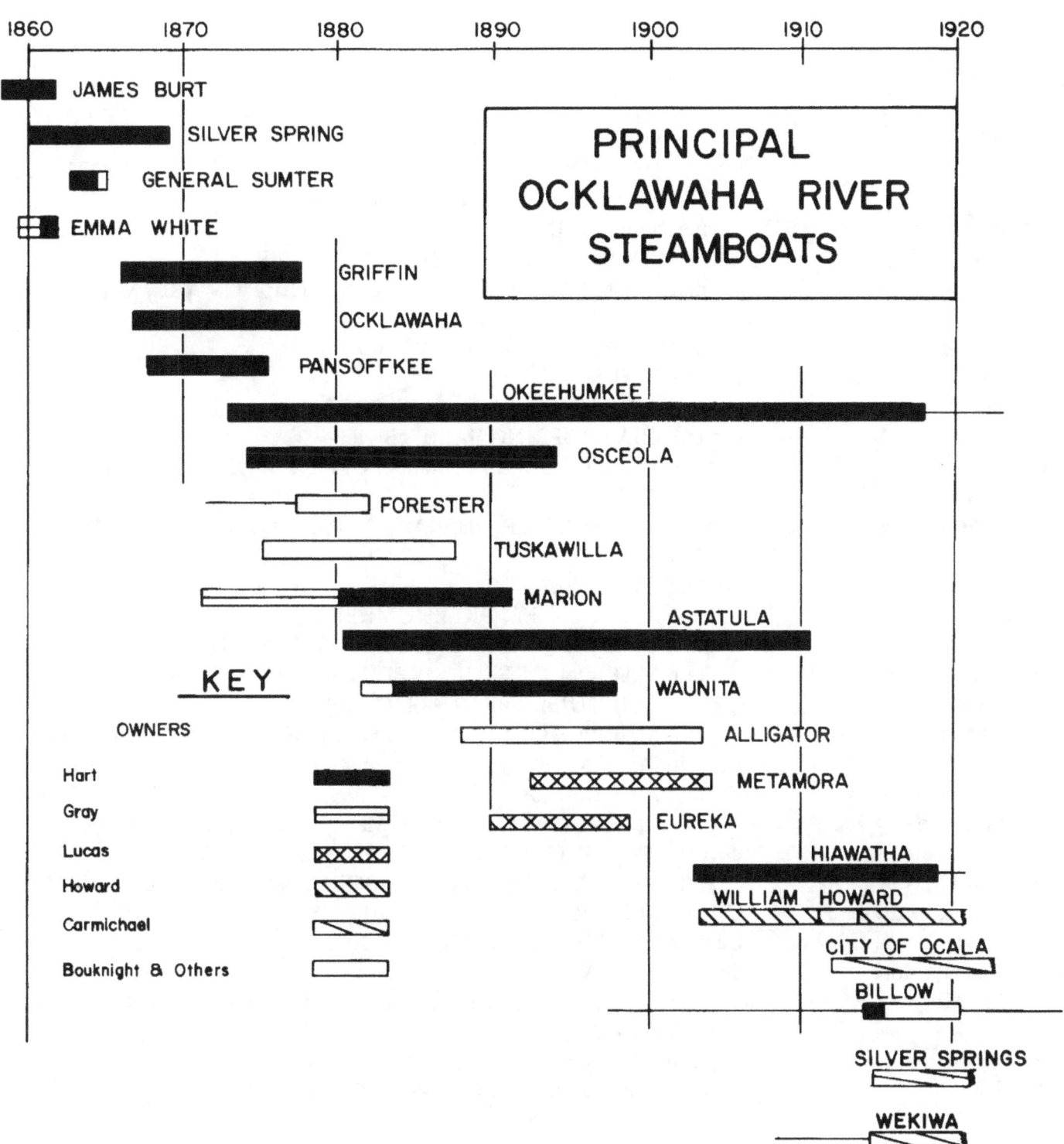

PRINCIPAL OCKLAWAHA RIVER STEAMBOATS

1860   1870   1880   1890   1900   1910   1920

JAMES BURT
SILVER SPRING
GENERAL SUMTER
EMMA WHITE
GRIFFIN
OCKLAWAHA
PANSOFFKEE
OKEEHUMKEE
OSCEOLA
FORESTER
TUSKAWILLA
MARION
ASTATULA
WAUNITA
ALLIGATOR
METAMORA
EUREKA
HIAWATHA
WILLIAM HOWARD
CITY OF OCALA
BILLOW
SILVER SPRINGS
WEKIWA

KEY

OWNERS

Hart
Gray
Lucas
Howard
Carmichael
Bouknight & Others

OCKLAWAHA PERSONAGES

Name	Function
Hubbard L. Hart	Entrepreneur, Proprietor Hart Line
Henry A. Gray	Owner EMMA WHITE, MARION, Hart Line Captain for ASTATULA, OSCEOLA, MARION - also rafting and pole barging
J. Ed Lucas	Owner, builder METAMORA, EUREKA
Dr. S. J. Bouknight	Owner, WAUNITA, TUSKAWILLA, FORESTER
J. Hatten Howard	Owner, builder WILLIAM HOWARD, SOPHIE HOWARD, MARY HOWARD
J. Hatten Howard, II	Owner, Captain WILLIAM HOWARD
Joe Pendleton	Captain MARION
J. E. Manucy	Captain ASTATULA, pole barging
George Allen	Captain SILVER SPRING, JAMES BURT
David A. Dunham	Supervisor Hart Shipyard, Captain GRIFFIN, OSCEOLA, ASTATULA, OCKLAWAHA
Joseph H. Smith	Captain scow PIONEER, FLORA, MARION - Owner, Captain WAUNITA, FLORA
G. A. Billings	Captain OCKLAWAHA
A. L. Rice	Captain PANSOFFKEE, OKEEHUMKEE
A. N. Edwards	Captain OSCEOLA, OKEEHUMKEE, MARION, TUSKAWILLA
W. H. Harrison	Captain MARION, OKEEHUMKEE, HIAWATHA
C. W. Howard	Captain ASTATULA, Builder ALLIGATOR
Richard J. Adams	Captain MARION, OCKLAWAHA, Hart Line Agent
A. F. Wade Mr. Mercier	Captain METAMORA
R. W. Thompson	Captain METAMORA
R. H. Thompson	Owner, Manager Hart Line Owner, Manager Hart Line
C. "Ed" Carmichael	Owner, CITY OF OCALA, SILVER SPRINGS, WEKIWA
William Carl Mason	Captain CITY OF OCALA and JOE BORDEN GLASS BOTTOM BOATS
Frederick E. Rossignol	Captain METAMORA
F. B. Lansing	Captain METAMORA, OKEEHUMKEE
Dr. Clarence B. More	Owner ALLIGATOR
Everett Lee Mills	Proprietor, Mills Steamboat Line, Captain SHARP SHOOTER, SHARP SHOOTER #2, HEL-KAT
Leland Mason	Captain SILVER SPRINGS "LEE M" JUNGLE CRUIS
Joe Borden	Proprietor JOE BORDEN GLASS BOTTOM BOATS

Clockwise — from top left: Captain David Dunham; Captain Richard Adams; Louise Mitchell, discoverer of the Hart Line records; C. Bradford Mitchell in HIAWATHA's pilot house. *Center* —genius of the Hart Line, Colonel Hubbard L. Hart.

United States Mail.

Change of Proprietorship.

CONCORD

COACHES,

GOOD

HORSES, &C.

PILATKA to TAMPA,

Via Orange Spring, Orange Lake, Ocala, Camp Izard, Augusta, Melendez, Pierceville, and Ft. Taylor.

Stages leave Pilatka and Tampa, Mondays and Thursdays, at 7 A. M., arriving at Tampa and Pilatka, (respectively,) the following Wednesdays and Saturdays; (resting at night, thereby affording Invalids a better opportunity for travelling,) connecting at Tampa with the

N. Orleans and Key West Steamers,

and at Pilatka with the Steam-Boats for Savannah and Charleston.

Also: Intersecting this line, is a Stage from Ocala, via Fleming- ton, Micanopy, and Newnansville, to Alligator.

EXTRA CARRIAGES & HORSES ON HAND,

at Pilatka, to convey Passengers to Micanopy, Flemington, Silver Spring, &c. &c.

ALL EXPRESS BUSINESS PROMPTLY ATTENDED TO.

OFFICE IN PILATKA, AT COL. J. O. DUVAL'S HOTEL.

July, 1855.

H. L. HART, Proprietor.

Hubbard L. Hart ran this cross-state stage coach service, and tied in with most forms of transportation then in existence. Note that "Pilatka" is now Palatka, Camp Izard was near Dunnellon, Melendez was the former seat of Benton County, today's Hernando County. Alligator is today's Lake City.

1871 sketches of early very crude, Ocklawaha River vessels.

Palatka-based vessels. *Above*, TRANSPORT, a local St. Johns River ferry that used a submerged cable for guidance on her journey across the river between Palatka and East Palatka. *Right*, a group on the PUTNAM, Captain David Dunham's excursion craft.

Local water transportation in the Palatka area. The steam launch PUTNAM was used on daylight trips.

At a Palatka wharf in the 1870s. *Above*, LOLLIE BOY, a local passenger and ferry vessel heads up a group of two other steam vessels. *Right*, LOLLIE BOY blows her stacks. Note small vessel in front and larger steamboat to the rear.

Above, ELIZA HANCOX at a St. Johns River wharf. *Below,* HARRY LEE, local Palatka excursion vessel. Tourists transferred from these vessels to Ocklawaha River steamboats.

The PRINCESS stopping for pictures on the Ocklawaha. Note large camera on the deck.

Ornate steam launch PRINCESS used in local Palatka daylight and excursions.

Above, towing sawed logs on a barge on the river in the 1920s. *Right,* OKAHUMKEE at a landing.

Alligator shooting on the Ocklawaha and St. Johns rivers. *Above,*
on the deck of the MARION,
1874. *Left,* on the MARION, also
in 1874.

Travelers' perils on the Ocklawaha River. Tree branches repeatedly strike the vessels. *Above, Harper's Weekly*, April 7, 1883. *Right, Scribner's* "Great South," November, 1874 (vessel is the MARION).

ON THE OCLAWAHA.—"LOOK OUT THAR!"

Ocklawaha River travel — *Above, unknown vessel, Directory,* (Jacksonville), 1885. *Left, Harper's Monthly* magazine, 1876.

THE OCKLAWAHA RIVER

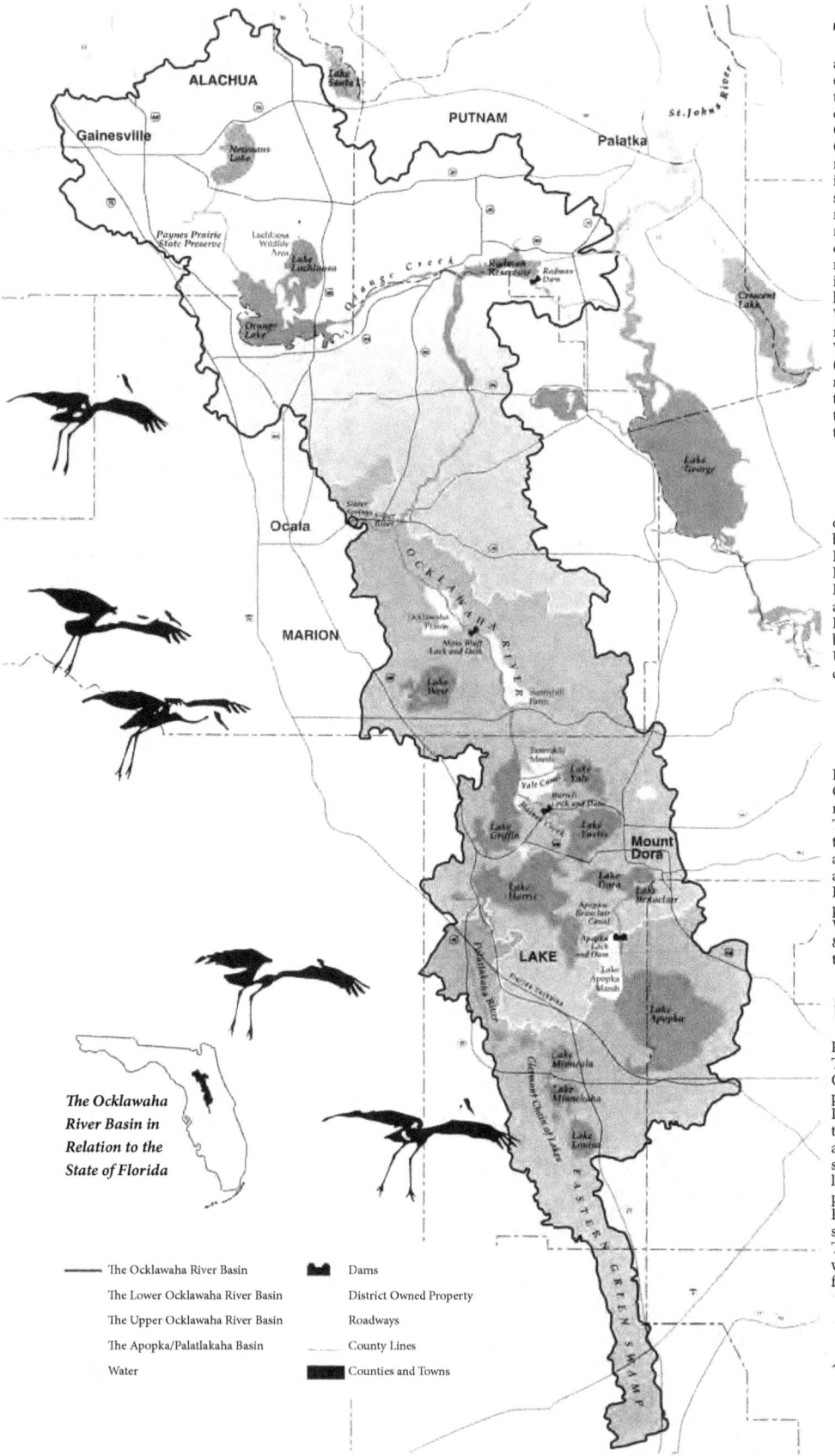

The Ocklawaha River is an inter-connected complex system and needs to be viewed as a whole - not as individual lakes or stretches of river. Changes in one section of the river system can have far-reaching effects further downstream. The Ocklawaha begins in Central Florida's Green Swamp, meanders 130 miles north to join the St. Johns River and is one of the few major rivers which flow from south to north. During the last century, the river has been changed by people to improve navigation, drain wetlands for farming and control flooding. As a result, this beautiful river and its lakes have experienced declines in water quality, changes in water flows and losses of wildlife habitat. The St. Johns River Water Management District is addressing the river system's problems through its Surface Water Improvement and Management (SWIM) program. SWIM is designed to restore and protect the rivers and lakes throughout Florida. This map shows the locations of restoration projects on the Ocklawaha.

The Lower Ocklawaha River Basin runs from State Road 40 north to the St. Johns River in Putnam County. This section of the river system still maintains much of its beauty described by author Marjorie Kinnan Rawlings half a century ago. Orange and Lochloosa Lakes, the Paynes Prairie State Preserve and the Cross Florida Greenway are all protected as "Outstanding Florida Waters." Plans for this segment of the river system are being patterned after the Lake Apopka and Upper Ocklawaha SWIM plans which are dealing with problems further upstream.

Further south is the Upper Ocklawaha River Basin, which includes the Ocklawaha Chain of Lakes in Lake County and the portion of the Ocklawaha River flowing from Lake Griffin north to the Silver River in Marion County. The District's SWIM program is working in this area to restore lake and wetland habitat and parts of the historic river channel that were abandoned earlier this century. Near the Silver River, the area changes from wide, marshy prairies to a picturesque, deep swamp forest. World-famous Silver Springs supplies about 80% of the flow in the Ocklawaha River as it travels north past State Road 40.

The southern-most section is where the Ocklawaha begins - two very different areas - the Palatlakaha River and Lake Apopka. The Palatlakaha River includes the Clermont Chain of Lakes and a small portion of the Green Swamp in southern Lake County. These lakes are designated by the state as "Outstanding Florida Waters" and as such, enjoy special protections. The other source - Lake Apopka - is the most polluted large lake in Florida. The District's SWIM program here includes the Marsh Flow-way Project which filters polluted lake water and sends cleaner water to the downstream lakes. The water management district is also working with agricultural interest to greatly reduce farm discharges into Lake Apopka.

The Ocklawaha River Basin in Relation to the State of Florida

The Ocklawaha River Basin

The Lower Ocklawaha River Basin

The Upper Ocklawaha River Basin

The Apopka/Palatlakaha Basin

Water

Dams

District Owned Property

Roadways

County Lines

Counties and Towns

1873 scenes on the Ocklawaha River, from "*Picturesque America*." *Top*, a cypress shingle mill. *Below*, a slight "obstruction."

A SLIGHT OBSTRUCTION IN THE OCKLAWAHA.

This may be Charles Seaver, Jr., noted stereo photographer. *Above, left,* shooting an "alligator." *Above, right,* "Breakfast is ready." *Below,* his small vessel was also used as a photo darkroom and river conveyance.

River scenes — *Above,* Fort Brooke Landing and settled area as seen from the river. *Left,* Graham's Landing, looking downstream.

Left, Rogers Cut at MP 84 (measured from the St. Johns). *Right,* the celebrated "narrows" on the Ocklawaha River, located at MP 14 measured from the Ocklawaha River mouth at the St. Johns.

Left, Ocklawaha River "Post Office" at Sharpe's Ferry Landing. *Right,* "Blasted Tree" on the Ocklawaha. Wood fuel used for river steamboats is stacked in the foreground.

Left, Narrow Pass above Eureka. *Right,* Graham's Landing on the Ocklawaha River.

Ocklawaha Scenery— *Above*, Sand Bluff Landing on the river. *Right*, Rogers Landing.

Right, the stereo photographer's little craft stopping at Jordan's Landing on the Ocklawaha River. *Below,* steam powered launch on the St. Johns and Ocklawaha Rivers.

OKEEHUMKEE lying to at Silver Springs. Passengers have disembarked and are waiting upon the return trip. Photo taken in 1900.

Tranquility at Silver Springs. Double-decked EUREKA (*left*) and daytime excursion boat WAHOO (*right*).

Above, WAHOO, daytime steam vessel at Silver Springs. *Below,* steam launch ELIZABETH at a wooden pier near Silver Springs.

Above, Silver Springs as the area developed during the steamboat era. Hotel is the Morgan House. Railroad station is at left. *Below*, Looking upstream from Silver Springs.

Riverboat traveling on the Ocklawaha River delivering and picking up mail from the river Post Office drop box while workers collect Spanish moss from trees along the riverbank.

All forms of transportation met at Silver Springs. Passenger trains meet the WILLIAM HOWARD and the HIAWATHA at Silver Springs. Stagecoach or carryall awaits passengers. Photo circa 1905.

Recreation activity as seen at Silver Springs in the Victorian era. *Above,* a glass bottom boat taking tourists to view the Springs. *Left,* a boating party on an outing.

Right, ROXIE advertisement, from promotional folder of the South Florida and Western Railway Co. 1882. *Below,* only known photo of the side-wheeler ROXIE, left, and TUSKAWILLA right, with steam launch in front. Perhaps taken at Leesburg, circa 1882. The ROXIE burned in late 1882 or 1883.

ST. JOHNS AND LAKE EUSTIS R'Y

THE GREAT LAKE REGION ROUTE,

OFFERS DAILY PASSENGER SERVICE

TO AND FROM — **ASTOR,** — AND ALL POINTS

On line of Road; thence by

NEW LAKE STEAMER ROXIE to and from LEESBURG

And all Intermediate Landings on LAKES EUSTIS and HARRIS; also connecting via **TAVUES** (the new town on Lake Dora) for points on adjacent lakes.

At **ASTOR**, connects with steamers via St. Johns River to and from Jacksonville and all points on the River.

THE MAIL STATIONS BETEEN ASTOR AND FORT MASON

— ARE —

BRYANT, RAVENSWOOD, GLENDALE
SUMMIT, ALTOONA, AND UMATILLA.

The distances being, from Astor to Summit, 13 miles; from Summit to Ravenswood, 4 miles; from Ravenswood to Altoona, 2 miles; from Altoona to Glendale, 2 miles; from Glendale to Umatilla, 1 mile; from Umatilla to Fort Mason, 4 miles.

The first five miles of country through which this road runs belongs to what is known as the Astor grant, being chiefly low pine lands, well timbered. From the Astor tract to Summit, a distance of 8 miles, it passes across the great Florida Scrub.

From Summit to Fort Mason the lands are high and rolling, with clear water lakes thickly scattered along the line of road, which for beauty cannot be surpassed by any of their kind in the State.

Altoona, the principal town or village, will ere long be one of the towns of importance in South Florida, where Northern visitors will find every inducement for pleasure or health.

From Lakes Harris and Eustis and the country around Fort Mason, the orange crops in winter and the vegetable crops in the spring are transported by the St. Johns and Lake Eustis Railway to the St. Johns River. Both crops are rapidly increasing.

GOOD HOTEL ACCOMMODATIONS

At Eustis, Tavues and Leesburg, and it is expected to erect a hotel at Astor, by November, '82.

W. J. JARVIS, *Superintendent.* W. H. TREADWELL, *Gen'l Freight and Pass'r Agent.*

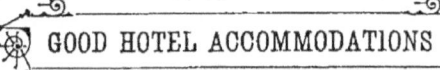

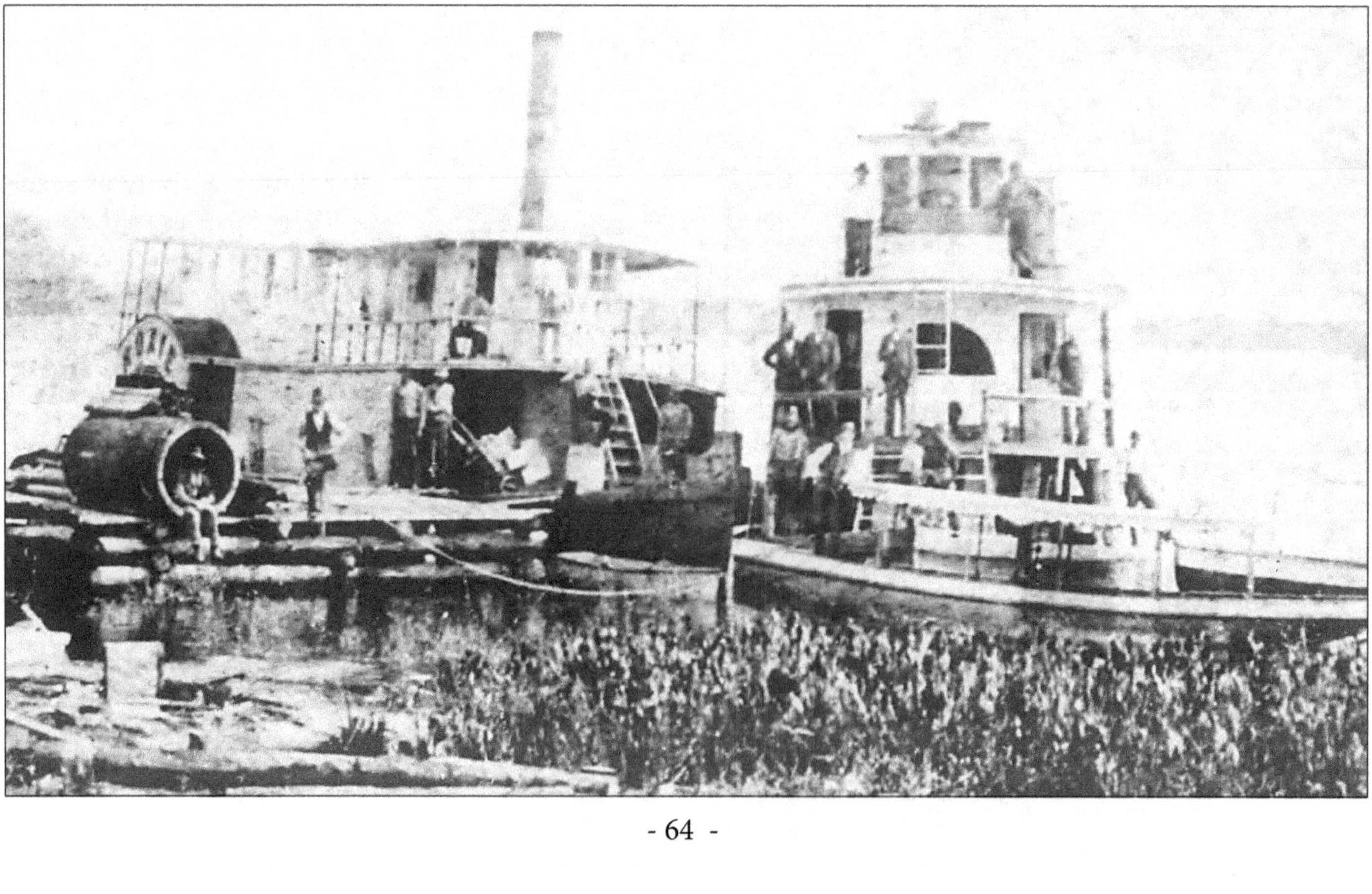

Early Hart Line OCKL-AWAHA — Note "twin" windows, single stairs. Pilot house was set at the front of the cabin deck. Shown here before second deck was extended forward and pilot house then placed atop second deck.

Two rare photos of an early OCKLAWAHA— Note rear cabin area and double windows.

Tourists posing for their portraits. Colonel Hubbard L. Hart is at top left near "O" in vessel name. Captain David Dunham is near "A" of name plate. Pilot house has been relocated atop the cabin deck. About half of this tourist group consists of doctors on a trip to Silver Springs.

Right, a St. Johns or Ocklawaha River scene as viewed from a steamer's deck. *Below,* the early Palatka-built Hart Line steamboat PANSOFFKEE, shown at a Palatka wharf.

Rare pictures found of GRIFFIN. *Left,* at Moss Bluff Landing, Upper Ocklawaha River. *Below,* "wooding up" at a river landing. Note excess freight stacked on top deck. Circa early 1870s.

MARION of the early 1870s. *Above,* at her home wharf in Palatka. *Below,* pictured at Iola Landing. Henry A. Gray was her owner and captain.

MARION was rebuilt exten-sively, perhaps in the early 1880s, and passed into Hart Line ownership. These pho- tos show her after rebuilding. In the lower photo, Captain Gray is seen near the pilot house door.

Bow view of MARION.

Tourists pose for their pictures. *Left,* on TUSKAWILLA, note artistic polygonal pilot house and circular leaded-glass cabin deck window. *Right,* tourists on ASTATULA in January, 1894.

TUSKAWILLA — *Right,* at Silver Springs, a group of tourists is posing with crew and dummy rifles. *Below,* at Gore's Landing. Note crude plank road, also decorative aspects of name on side of vessel.

TUSKAWILLA — *Left,* tourists having their pictures taken. Note TUSKAWILLA's distinctive name board lettering and polygonal pilot house. *Right,* at Silver Springs. A group of tourists is posing for their pictures. Note artistic balusters.

OKLAWAHA RIVER !
FROM JACKSONVILLE
TO
Palatka, Silver Springs, Leesburg, Okeehumkee,
AND ALL INTERMEDIATE LANDINGS ON THE ST JOHN'S AND OKLAWAHA RIVERS.

THE STEAMER TUSKAWILLA,

A: N. EDWARDS, Master,

Will leave S. G. SEARING & CO.'S WHARF, foot of Pine street, every THURSDAY MORNING, at 8 o'clock.

For Freight or Passage, apply to

S. G. SEARING & CO.,
General Freight and Passenger Agents,
Jacksonville, Fla.

Dr. S. J. Bouknight and his brother had interests in three Ocklawaha River steamboats, the WAUNITA, FORESTER, and TUSKAWILLA. *Above,* an 1878 advertisement of the TUSKAWILLA, and *right,* an early 1880s advertisement from a tourist guide.

— 48 —

BOUKNIGHT'S DAILY LINE
OF
OCKLAWAHA STEAMERS;

Leaving Palatka Daily, 9.30 A. M.,

FOR
SILVER SPRINGS.

TIME OF ROUND TRIP 35 HOURS.

THE new and elegant steamers "Waunita," having superb passenger accomodations, and the popular steamer "Tuskawilla," will leave Palatka daily at 9.30 A. M. for Silver Springs.

CONNECTING ON
Tuesdays, Thursdays and Saturdays,
WITH
Steamer "Forrester" for Leesburgh,

and all intermediate landings on the Ocklawaha River, Lakes Griffin, Eustis and Harris.

Tickets and information to be had at

General Office, LEMON STREET,
OR AT
——) LEVE & ALDEN'S Offices. (——

Left, WAUNITA, at Samuel Agnew's turpentine still, "300 barrels per month capacity." *Below*, WAUNITA Sanford (wharf on Lake Monroe). CHATTAHOOCHEE, H. B. Plant's large steel-hulled sternwheeler at left.

The WAUNITA of the mid-1880s. *Above,* at Silver Springs with the OKAHUMKEE. *Below,* with ASTATULA at Sanford (Lake Monroe) on the St. Johns River. Note railroad track on wharf.

The **ALLIGATOR of 1888.** Never a great factor in the river trade, she was owned by Dr. Clarence B. Moore of Philadelphia who used her in his archaeological pursuits along the Ocklawaha.

Right, 1875 advertisement of Hart Line Ocklawaha River trips. *Below,* Hart Line competitor Henry Gray's MARION—1878 advertisement.

OKEEHUMKEE — leaving Silver Springs circa 1886.

OKEEHUMKEE — *Above,* leaving Silver Springs circa 1886. Photo and one on preceding page taken by George Barker, award winning photographer. *Below,* a reconfigured OSCE-OLA showing cabins extended to rear of stack, at Silver Springs.

Hart's OSCEOLA — *Above,* with a heavy passenger load at a river landing. *Left,* at Silver Springs. Note that cabins have not yet been added.

Above, Winter visitors posing on OSCEOLA. *Below,* Crew of OSCEOLA has their picture taken by George Barker, winter, 1886.

Above, ASTATULA on May 8, 1894. Captain Henry Gray is second from left on top deck. *Below,* Florida visitors on ASTATULA, May, 1897.

Captain Henry Gray on top deck (near letter "A") two years before his death.

ASTATULA at an Ocklawaha River landing.

ASTATULA — *Above,* in mid-stream on the Ocklawaha River. *Below,* at Palatka wharf. Final version with complete row of cabins and top side railings.

EUREKA (left) at Silver Springs, OKEEHUMKEE at right.

EUREKA at Silver Springs, two configurations are shown, both other than handsome.

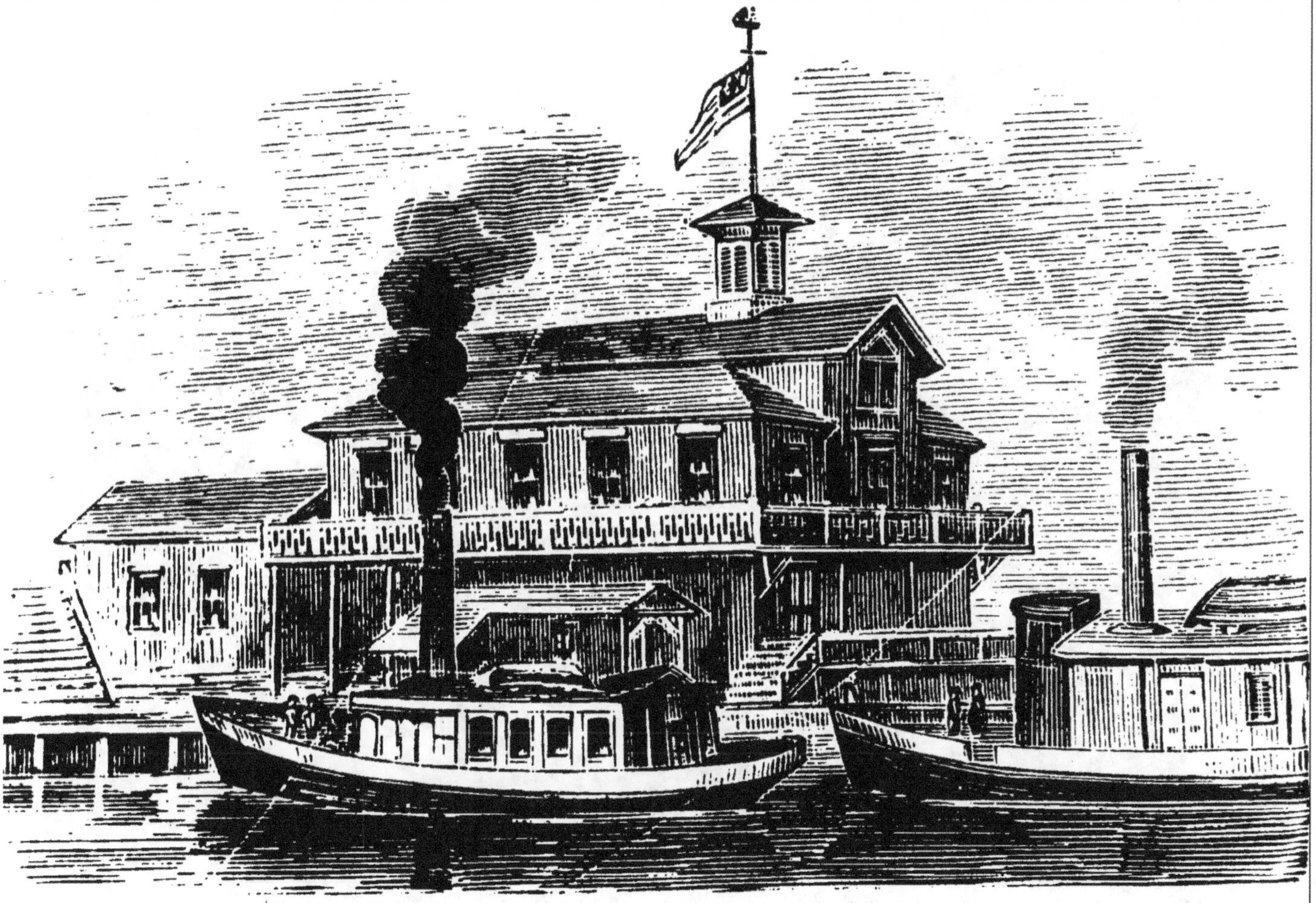

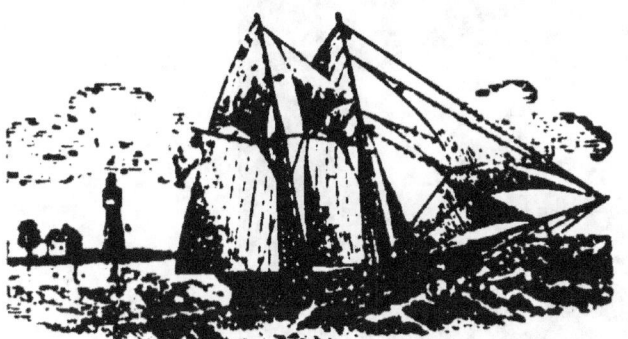

Captain Lucas' Boathouse and Wharf.

Above, **sketch of Captain Ed Lucas' Palatka boathouse and wharf. *Below,* advertisement for Captain Lucas' boat livery. Lucas built and owned the METAMORA.**

THOS. DARDIS AND J. E. LUCAS,

Steam Yacht, Sail & Row Boats

Of every description and size

For hire on reasonable terms by the hour, day, or trip.; also

RIFLES, GUNS, FISHING TACKLE AND LINES.

Boathouse opposite the Larkin House,

Palatka, Florida.

Above, 1895 view of METAMORA. Note polygonal pilothouse, absence of name lettering on side. *Below,* in the early 1900s, rounding a bend on the Ocklawaha, steam being exhausted.

The early 1900s see META-MORA at Silver Springs, *above*. *Left*, as underway on the river, inboard paddlewheel churning away.

METAMORA meeting a train at Silver Springs.

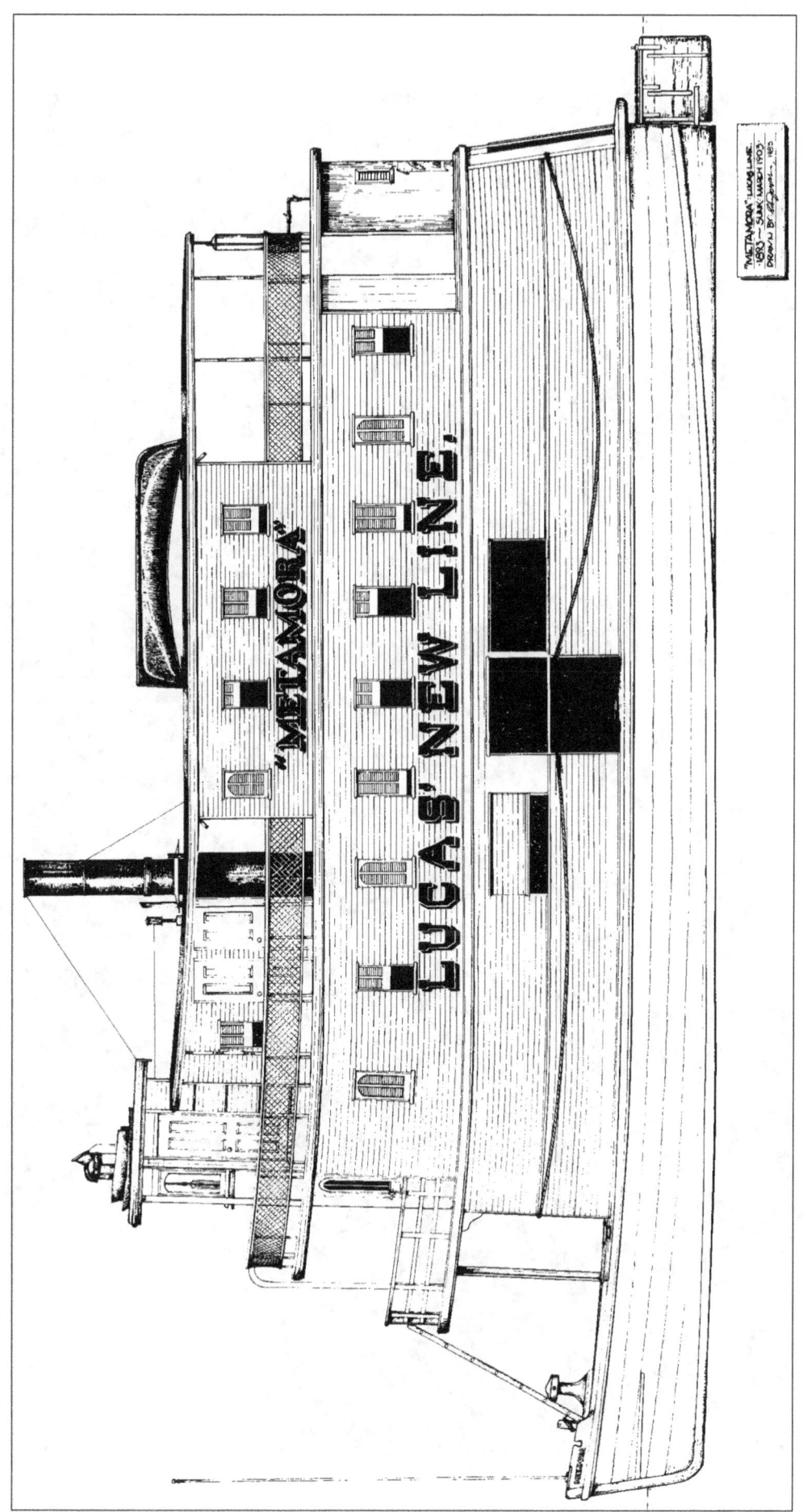

"METAMORA" LUCAS LINE.
1893 — SIDE, MARCH 1903
DRAWN BY [signature], 1983

METAMORA stopping for her portrait.

METAMORA poses in the Ocklawaha River.

The only fatalities on the Ocklawaha River occurred on METAMORA in 1903 when she hit a snag. Shown *above* at the accident scene—steam launch is off-loading passengers. *Below,* partially sunk in Palatka. Vessel at left is the EULALIA.

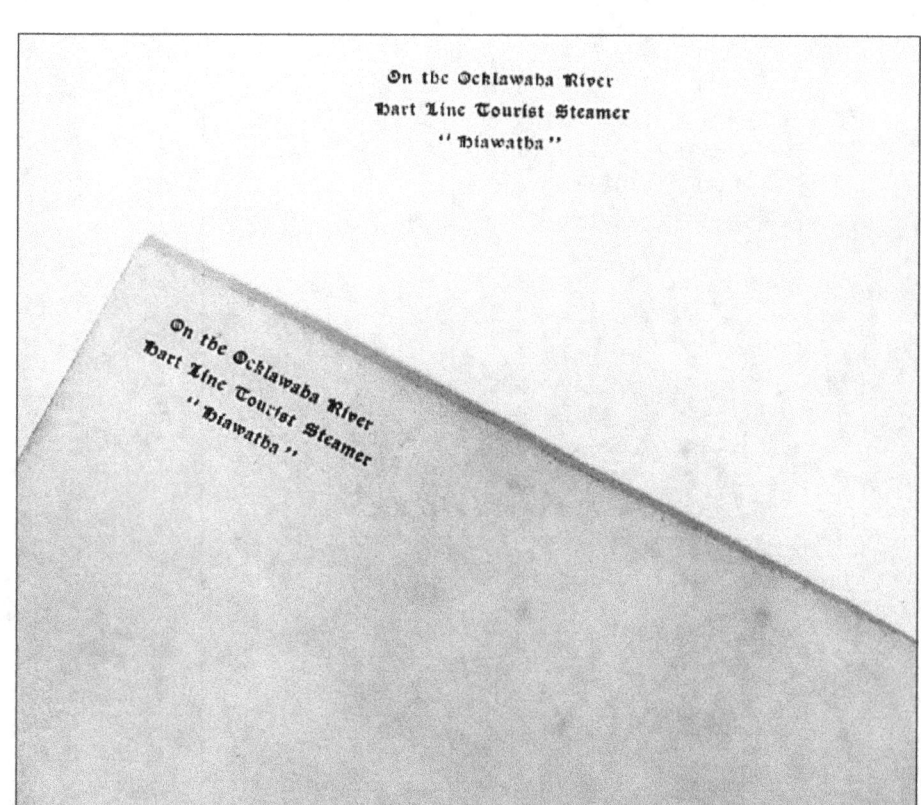

On the Ocklawaha River
Hart Line Tourist Steamer
"Hiawatha"

Right, stationery used aboard the HIAWATHA.

HART'S DAILY LINE

OF

OCKLAWAHA RIVER STEAMERS.

Str. Okeehunkee,   Str. Osceola,

CAPT. A. L. RICE,   CAPT. D. A. DUNHAM,

Leave PALATKA at 9 A. M.

FOR SILVER SPRING, LEESBURG, AND OKEEHUNKEE.

H. L. HART, *Proprietor and Agent.*

Tickets on sale with **LEVE & ALDEN**, 271 Broadway, New York, and at their Agencies.

Choice Oranges from the H. L. Hart Grove shipped to order to all points North.

Left, 1880 advertisement (misspelling and all).

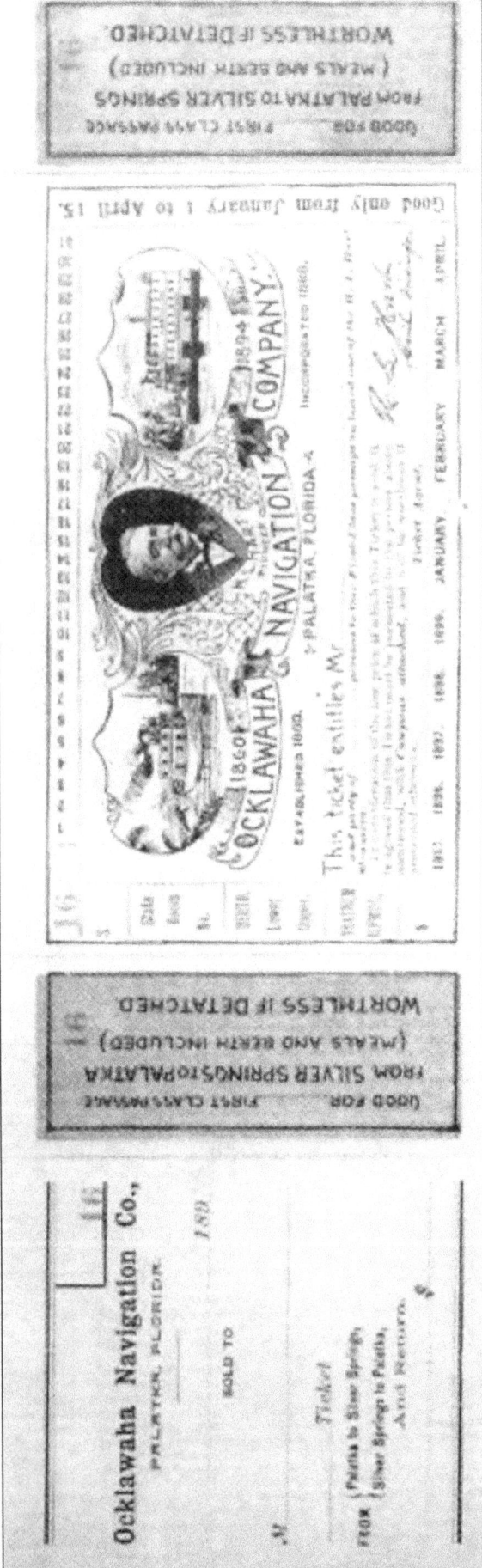

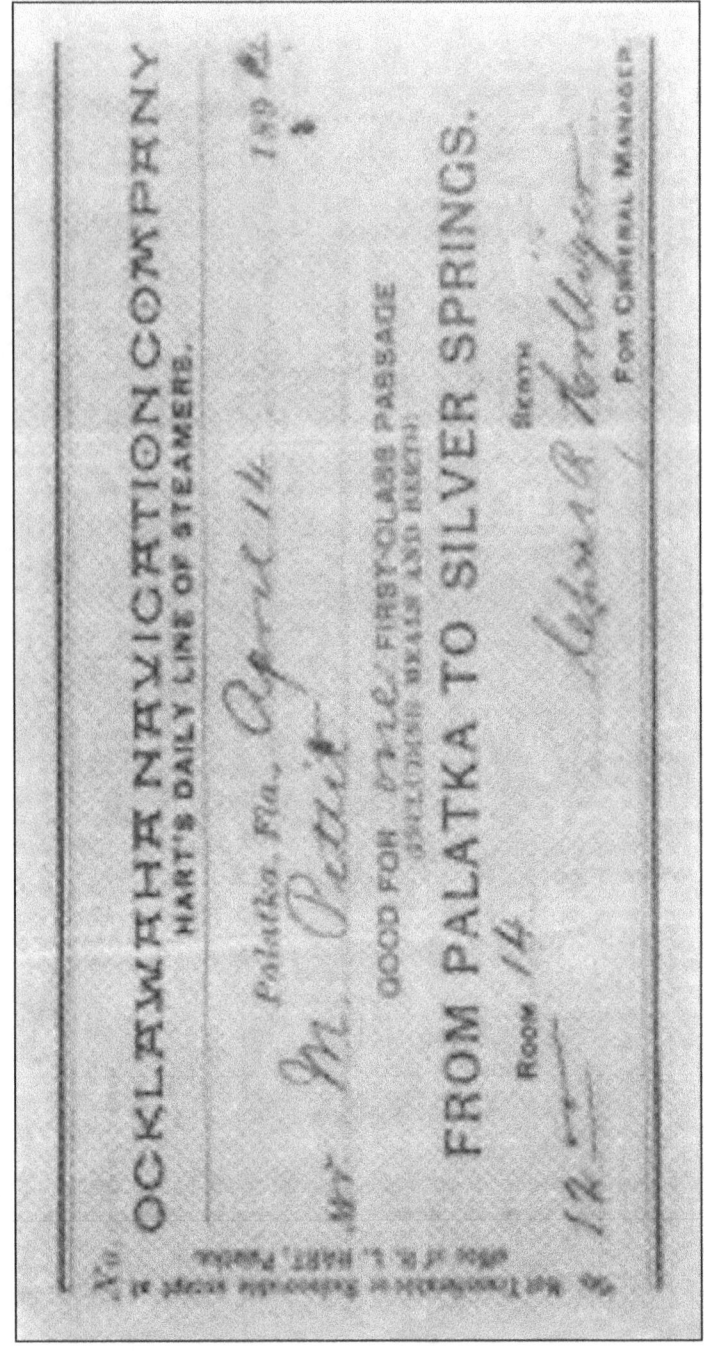

Hart Line Tickets — *Top* — Left part of agent's copy; vertical portion (both) is collected for each end of the round trip. Center portion with photo is retained by passenger. "Yratnemilpmoc" is "complimentary" spelled backwards. *Right,* one-way ticket, from Palatka to Silver Springs.

Following is a copy of the 1900 Hart Line promotional brochure. The dark red covers have been omitted due to difficult reproduction.

Ocklawaha River and Silver Springs Daily Line.

A STEAMBOAT for the Ocklawaha River and Silver Springs leaves Hart's wharf, Palatka, daily, Sunday excepted, at 12.15 noon or after arrival of trains from St. Augustine and Jacksonville. Returning leaves Silver Springs daily, Monday excepted, after arrival of trains from Tampa, Ocala and Jacksonville, via F. C. & P. R. R. and Plant System R. R. The tourist on morning trains can make close connection at Palatka with the steamboats for a round trip to Silver Springs up and down the Ocklawaha, resuming his journey on his return to the point of his destination.

State rooms and berths can be obtained on the boat at time of sailing, or can be secured in advance by letter or telegram, directed to the office in Palatka.

How to Reach Palatka.

SCHEDULE OF ARRIVAL OF TRAINS AND STEAMBOATS, CORRECTED TO FEBRUARY 15, 1900.

Daily via J. T. & K. W. Ry., Plant System, South Bound, 11.50 a.m., 2.00 p.m., 6.00 p.m.

Daily via J. T. & K. W. Ry., Plant System, North Bound, 2.40 a.m., 5.05 p.m.

Via East Coast Line, South Bound, 9.10 a.m., 12.05 p.m.

Via "   "   "   North Bound, 9.10 a.m., 5.37 p.m.

Via Georgia Southern & Florida, South Bound, 9.40 a.m., 10 p.m.

Via Florida Southern Ry., Plant System, East Bound, 10 a.m.

Via Beach & Miller Steamers, South Bound, 3 p.m., Tuesdays, Thursdays, Saturdays.

Via Beach & Miller Steamers, North Bound, 1.30 a.m., Mondays, Wednesdays, Fridays.

Via Clyde Line River Steamers, South Bound, 8.45 p.m., Sundays, Tuesdays, Thursdays.

Via Clyde Line River Steamers, North Bound, 8 p.m., Mondays, Wednesdays, Fridays.

W. C. HARGROVE, G. P. A.,   A. S. THOMPSON,

HART'S BLOCK, PALATKA, FLA.   TRAVELLING PASSENGER AGENT.

MOUTH OF THE OCKLAWAHA RIVER.

A CAPTAIN OF AN OCKLAWAHA STEAMBOAT.

PALATKA.

Palatka is a well-known tourist resort, a railroad, steamboat and commercial center, at the headwaters of ocean navigation, with six lines of railroad radiating therefrom.

The tourist is enabled from this central point to reach quickly any part of the state, and to embrace the Ocklawaha River and Silver Springs as a connecting water link in his itinerary. This city offers to the visitor a dry and balmy climate, neighboring lakes, rivers and creeks for short boating trips, for fishing and hunting, pure soft spring water from the range of hills bounding the town on the west, and has one of the largest and best hotels in the state.

THE OCKLAWAHA RIVER.

This remarkable river, rising in a chain of large lakes, flows about one hundred and seventy-five miles to the St. Johns.

Leaving Palatka the steamboats pass up the St. Johns river twenty-five miles, where they enter the old forests of the Ocklawaha, of towering cypress, pine and palmetto, clad in vines and air plants, and reach the terminus at Silver Springs, about one hundred and thirty-five miles. The flora and fauna of the entire route excite continuous interest, and the ever winding current abounds in alligators and turtles. Semi-tropical birds of fine plumage add to the wildness of the picturesque scenery. A round trip from

Palatka to Silver Springs affords a view by daylight of all the most beautiful parts of the river. No tourist has seen the most beautiful natural scenery of Florida if he has not sailed up and down the swift and mystical current of this romantic stream, one of the most famous rivers of the world that have attained distinction, and one of the most popular routes on the American continent.

OCKLAWAHA STEAMBOATS.

The transparent and marvelous waters of Silver Springs run for nine miles, pouring into the Ocklawaha a crystal stream, over which the steamboats pass, so mirror like that fish, turtles, and all living things therein seem as if suspended in air.

These steamboats are strongly built especially for this river, and their unique construction is such that they are marvels of comfort and steadiness of motion.

Their state rooms accommodate fifty passengers. They are commanded by skilful captains and stalwart, faithful pilots of long experience on this river.

The kindness and courtesy of the officers, and the generous bill of fare as well as the memorable incidents of the trip, have been universally commended.

The most delicate tourist finds an outing on this river, with its ever changing scenes, and with its tonic air laden with balsamic odors of the forest, an inspiration to health and good cheer.

TAMING THE 'GATOR ON THE OCKLAWAHA.

River and plantation melodies are usually rendered by the colored crew at night.

Gen. U. S. Grant, on his return from a tour of the world, pronounced the Ocklawaha the most charming of rivers, and this trip one of the most pleasing events of his life.

RAYMOND AND WHITCOMB TOURISTS ON THE OCKLAWAHA.

Rev. Dr. Cuyler says that "the visitor to Florida who misses a trip up the Ocklawaha on one of these famous river steamboats fails to behold the greatest attraction of the state."

Mrs. Henry Ward Beecher exclaimed, "this is my fifth trip on the river, and I would not miss it for anything."

THE NIGHT SCENES.

Most effective of all is the Ocklawaha by torchlight. The negro pilots kindle their lightwood flambeaux. The resinous yellow flames light up the banks with their dense growth of cypress, palmetto, pine, gum tree, the slender palm, the flowering horse-chestnut, the bay-tree and the blossoming dogwood, the magnolia,

"WOODING UP" ON THE OCKLAWAHA.

and the rododendron, the woodbine, the orchid and sweet-scented jasmine, together with rank tropical water lilies fringing the water line.

And now behold the illuminated glory of the towering palmetto, the mighty vine-twined cypress, and the lofty pine!

Their tossing, waving, festooning mosses become silvered garlands. Their spreading tops are crowned with a foliage of splendor. The dark water sparkles with amethysts. It is a wierd and glorious vision.

The region of the Ocklawha is rich in fossil remains of the mastodon, the hippopotami and

other varieties of animal life, and at the "bone-yard," so-called, near Silver Springs, have been discovered the bones of whales, the vertabrae of which were nineteen inches in diameter, and the petrified remains of a marine monster ninety feet long and five feet in diameter. There are many Indian sand mounds along this river, containing ornamental and useful implements of stone and copper.

ASCENDING THE OCKLAWAHA.

SILVER SPRINGS.

Silver Springs are the outlets of an underground river that daily discharges into the Okla-waha River three hundred million gallons of water. These springs are contained in five lime-stone basins bearing names suggested by the hues of the rock and the variegated mosses therein. The largest basin is about eighty-five feet deep by two hundred wide, and the water is so transparent that a dime thrown to the bottom can be clearly seen, and all objects placed in this water immediately take on an irridescent glow.

To look into these mysterious depths forcibly reminds one of Jules Verne's "Ten Thou-and Leagues Under the Sea."

But no pen can describe this great natural wonder of the American Continent; the tra-ditional and veritable fountain of youth of Ponce de Leon.

TRAVEL VIA
Lucas' New Line
OCKLAWAHA RIVER and SILVER SPRINGS
STEAMER,
PLYING BETWEEN
Palatka and the Famous and Popular Silver Springs.

The New, Fast and Popular Steamer
METAMORA,
"Queen of the Ocklawaha River,"
A. F. WADE, Captain,

Surpassing all other Steamers on this river (excepting none) in her equipment, both as to her Large and Elegant Staterooms, Meals and Service. (We invite comparison.) We make OUR TABLE A SPECIALTY, supplying it with the VERY BEST the market affords, and give you a DAYLIGHT SAIL DOWN THE SILVER SPRINGS and OCKLAWAHA RIVER.

Do not be deceived. The METAMORA is the only New Steamer not built over or added to, this being her second season.

SEE OTHER SIDE FOR SCHEDULES.

For Tickets, Staterooms and full information apply to all Tourist, Hotel and Railroad Ticket Offices at principal points, or telegraph or write to

J. E. LUCAS, Gen. Mgr.,   JAS. P. BEALE, P. Agt.,   W. H. LUCAS, G. T. P. A.
Palatka, Fla.   St. Augustine, Fla.   Jacksonville, Fla.

THE DA COSTA PRINTING HOUSE, JACKSONVILLE, FLA.

LUCAS' NEW LINE
ST. JOHNS, OCKLAWAHA RIVER and SILVER SPRINGS STEAMER.

Schedule to and from Silver Springs.

Stmr. Metamora

Leaves Palatka Mondays, Wednesdays and Fridays at 12.30 p. m. or on arrival of trains from Jacksonville and St. Augustine, arriving at SILVER SPRINGS 9.30 a. m. next morning, connecting with trains for Ocala, Tampa and Jacksonville.

Returning:

Leaves Silver Springs 10.30 a. m., or on arrival of trains from Ocala and Tampa, leaving Ocala 9.52 a. m., Tuesdays, Thursdays and Saturdays, giving a DAYLIGHT SAIL DOWN THE SILVER SPRINGS and OCKLAWAHA RIVER.

WAIT for the ABOVE DAYS and STEAMER if you wish to see the MOST and get the VALUE of your MONEY.

THE METAMORA RUNS ON SCHEDULE TIME.

FROM PALATKA TO

LANDINGS.	MILES.	LANDINGS	MILES
Hart's Grove	1	Payne's Landing	73
Rolleston	2½	Iola	75
San Mateo	5	Well's Landing	77
Dunn's Creek	7	Forty-foot Bluff	78
Murphy Island	8½	Rough and Ready Cut	79
Buffalo Bluff	9½	Ed Moore Cut-off	81
Satsuma	18	Log Landing	85
Nashua	19	Eureka Cut-off	86
Roots Wharf	20	Eureka	87
Three Sisters	22	Cyprus Gate	87½
Welaka	25	Sunday Bluff	94
Mouth of Ocklawaha River	25½	Twin Cyprus	95
Boyd's Creek	29	Bear Tree	97
Bear Island	31	Star Island	98
Davenport	32	Hogan's Landing	100
Poor Man's Labor Pinner's	37	Pin Hook	100¼
Narrows	39	Hell's Half Acre	101
Freeborn's Cut	39½	Park's Landing	102
Riverside	40	Dodger Island	102½
Deep Creek	43	Gore's Landing	103
Jack Gates	44	Brush Heap	103½
Turkey Creek	45	Straits of "Dardin	
Blue or Salt Spring	48	Kennels"	104
Cedar Landing	50	Osceola's Old Field	105
Tuskawilla Cut	52	Duriso's Landing	106
Sims Landing	54½	Roger's Cut	113
Honey Bee Log	54½	Stuart Creek	114
Fort Brooke	58	Chitty's Avenue	115
Jordon's Landing	58½	Palmetto Grove	116
Orange Creek, (Orange		Long's Landing	117
Springs Landing	59	Grahamville	118
Needles Eye	60	Howard's Landing	119
Gray's Cut	61	McKroski's Old Field	122
McBride s Landing	61½	Delk's Bluff	125
McBride s Cut	62	Silver Spring Run	126
Indian Bluff	63½	White Oak Landing	127
Twin Palmettos	64½	Helvington's Landin	129
Long Reach	65	Rodger's Grove	130
Big Eddy	67	Marshall's Landing	131
Machetts Shoals	68	Pasteur's Landing	132
Crowningshield	69	Robinson's Landing	134
Hart's Secession Camp	69½	Turpentine Still Landing	134¼
		Jocob's Wells	134½

SILVER SPRINGS 135 MILES.

OCKLAWAHA RIVER.

HART'S LINE—LUCAS' LINE, Consolidated.

SEASON 1899.

THE OKEEHUMKEE.

M. M. VICKERS PRESS, PALATKA.

No Tourist

CAN AFFORD TO VISIT FLORIDA
WITHOUT TAKING A TRIP
ON THE WILD, WONDERFUL
AND CROOKED

OCKLAWAHA RIVER

WHICH HAS 999 TURNS
FROM ITS MOUTH TO
THE FAMOUS xxx

SILVER SPRING

The Beauties of Which
Cannot be Described
but must be Seen.

The finely equipped steamers,

Okeehumkee

and Metamora

Have each 26 neatly furnished State Rooms and can accommodate 60 first-class passengers.

Their Tables equal those of the best hotels in the State.

Their State and Toilet Rooms have a thorough system of plumbing.

Their wide and comfortable berths have the best of spring beds and hair mattresses.

The Palatka Heights pure, soft, crystal-clear Spring Water, is used on these boats.

J. E. LUCAS,
General Manager,
St. J. & O. R. S. B. Co.,
Palatka, Fla.

R. H. THOMPSON,
General Manager
Hart's Line.
Palatka, Fla.

W. C. HARGROVE, G. P. A.,
Palatka, Florida.

Schedule

JANUARY—During the month of January, 1899, a steamer will leave Palatka at 9 o'clock a. m. on the 9th, 11th, 16th, 18th, 23d, 25th, 27th, and 30th, reaching Silver Spring at 8:30 the morning after leaving Palatka.

Returning will leave Silver Spring at 9 o'clock a. m. on the 10th, 12th, 17th, 19th, 24th, 26th, 28th, and 31st, reaching Palatka at midnight the same day.

FEBRUARY—Leave Palatka at 9 o'clock a. m. on the 1st, 3d, 6th, 8th, 10th, 13th, 15th, and 17th.

Returning, leave Silver Spring at 9 o'clock a. m. on the 2d, 4th, 7th, 9th, 11th, 14th, 16th, 18th.

After February 18th, at 9 o'clock a. m., a boat will leave Palatka every day except Sunday. Leave Silver Spring every day except Monday

This schedule enables the tourist to see the most attractive parts of the Ocklawaha and the indescribable Silver Spring Run by daylight, both going and coming.

A classic view of OKAHUMKEE at a landing.

These views are of OKAHUMKEE (OKEEHUMKEE) as in her early days. *Left,* at Silver Springs with a group of winter visitors. *Below,* at a way landing.

Two views of OKEEHUMKEE before top rear cabins for passengers were added. Note how inboard paddlewheel churns water at full speed.

OKEEHUMKEE—at landings, "wooding up"—Note chicken or livestock coop at top rear. Wooden shutters protected windows from tree branches when vessel was underway.

Above, OKAHUMKEE "wooding up" at a landing. *Below,* tourists posing at a river landing aboard the OKAHUMKEE.

Above, side view of OKEEHUMKEE. Note shuttered windows. *Below,* February 26, 1895 photo of OKEEHUMKEE at Palatka.

Above, OKEEHUMKEE in 1894. Note "Queen of the Ocklawaha River" name board atop pilot house. *Below,* at Silver Springs. Cabins now extend entire length of vessel.

**OKEEHUMKEE posing for her portrait when making
a critical bend on the Ocklawaha River, circa 1910.**

**Final repose—OKEEHUMKEE at Hart's Point, East
Palatka, in mid-1930s. Dismantled soon afterwards.**

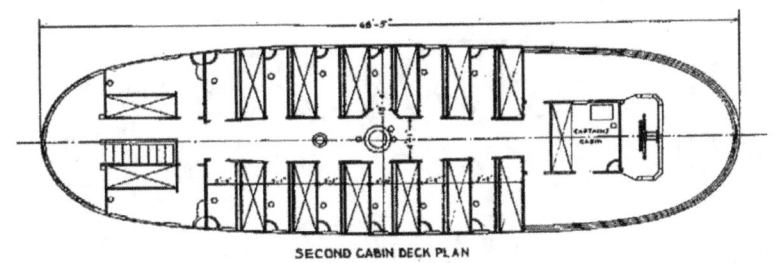

SECOND CABIN DECK PLAN

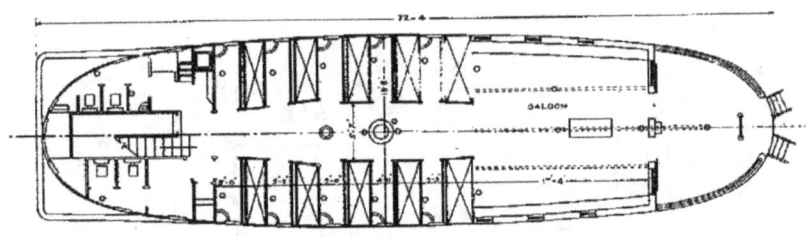

FIRST CABIN DECK PLAN

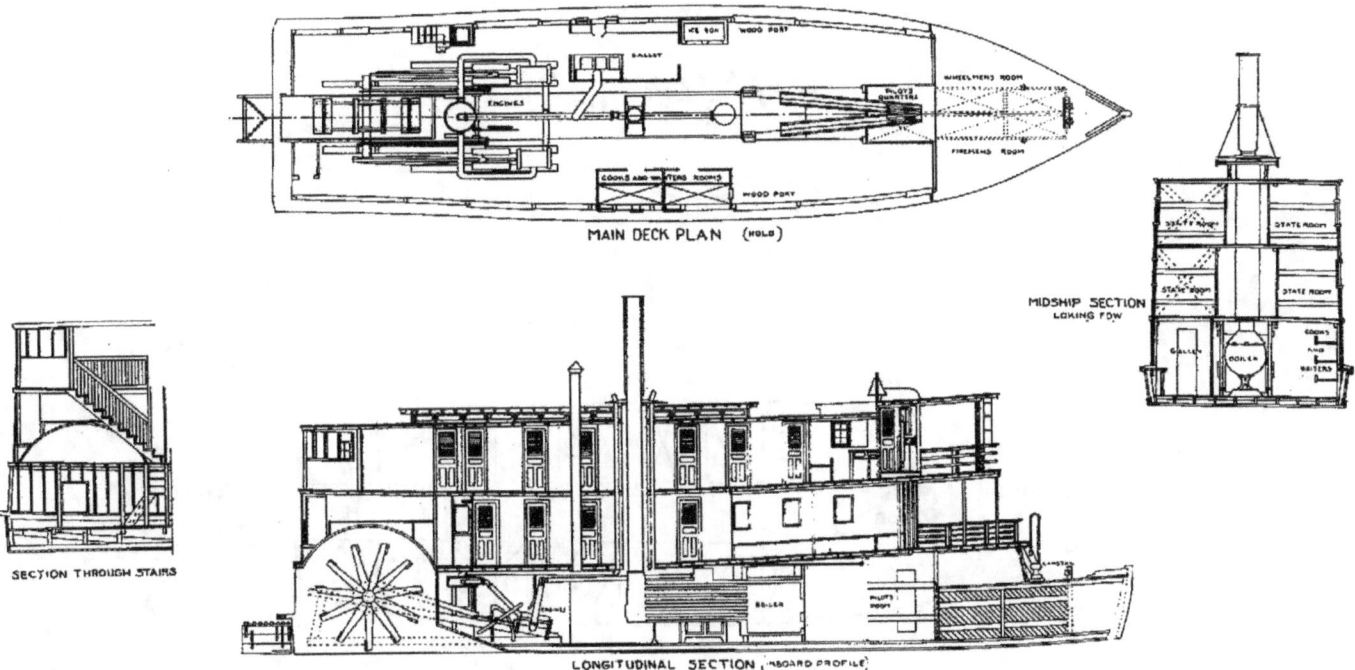

MAIN DECK PLAN (HOLD)

MIDSHIP SECTION
LOOKING FOW

SECTION THROUGH STAIRS

LONGITUDINAL SECTION (INBOARD PROFILE)

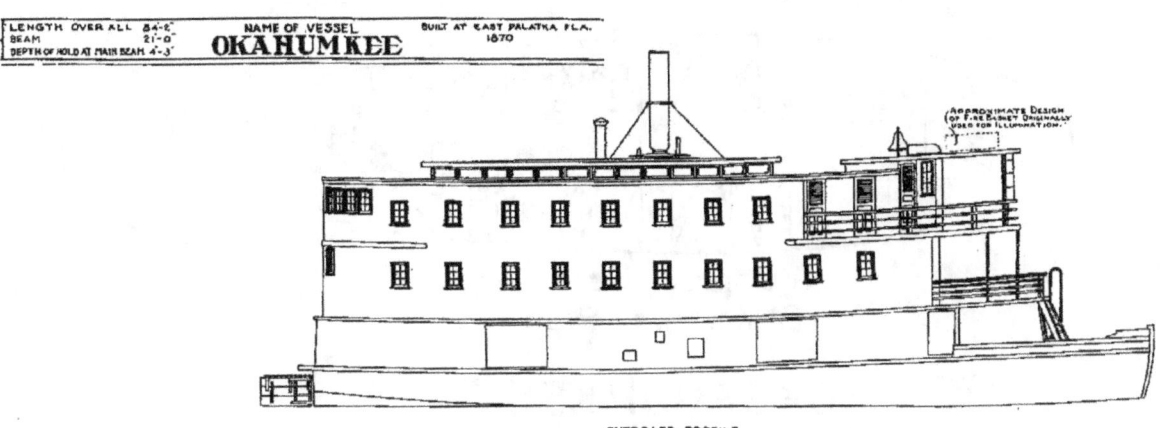

LENGTH OVER ALL 84-5"	NAME OF VESSEL	BUILT AT EAST PALATKA FLA.
BEAM 21-0"	OKAHUMKEE	1870
DEPTH OF HOLD AT MAIN BEAM 4-3"		

APPROXIMATE DESIGN
OF FIRE BASKET ORIGINALLY
USED FOR ILLUMINATION.

OUTBOARD PROFILE

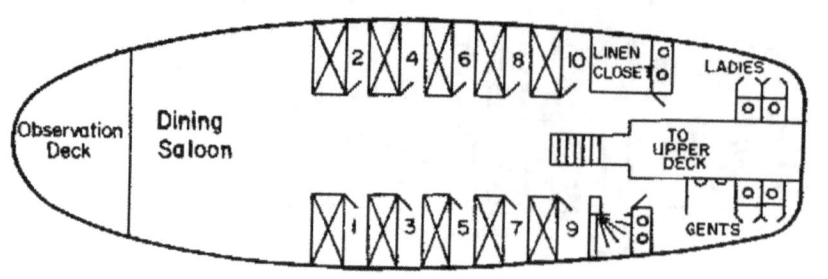

Saloon
Deck

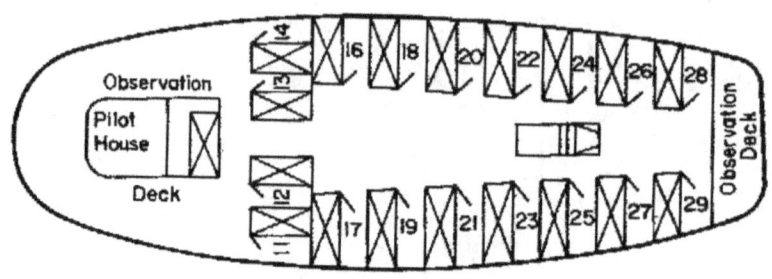

Upper Deck
Stateroom Plan

"HIAWATHA"

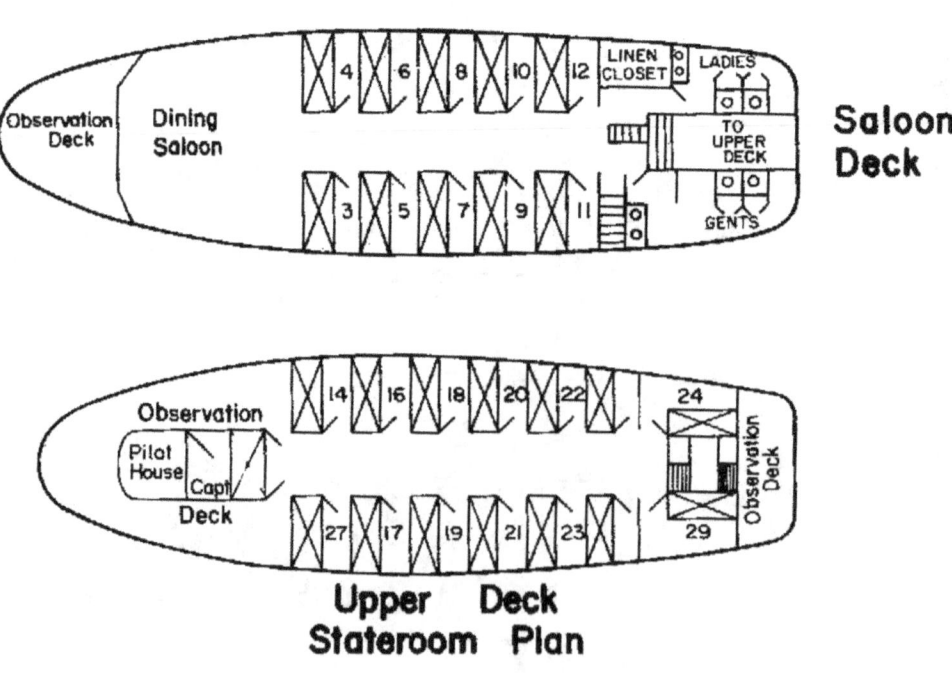

Saloon
Deck

Upper Deck
Stateroom Plan

" OKEEHUMKEE "

"Queen of the Ocklawaha"—HIAWATHA, Hart Line vessel in the 1910s.

**HIAWATHA—only twin-stacked Hart Line vessel, shown
here in the 1900s with a full passenger load of tourists.**

Above, post card, faked "night" shot of HIAWATHA showing how pine knots 'illuminate' at night. Actually a day view is used and retouched extensively. *Below,* post card, the Hart flag has been touched in as has the bird at lower right.

HIAWATHA—*Above,* sunk at Hart's Point, East Palatka, circa 1920s. *Below,* at Hart's Point, 1935. She slowly disintegrated there and was finally removed in 1979.

Above, HIAWATHA as a forgotten wreck at Hart's Point, East Palatka. *Left*, 1954 view of abandoned HIAWATHA, Robby Robson at bow.

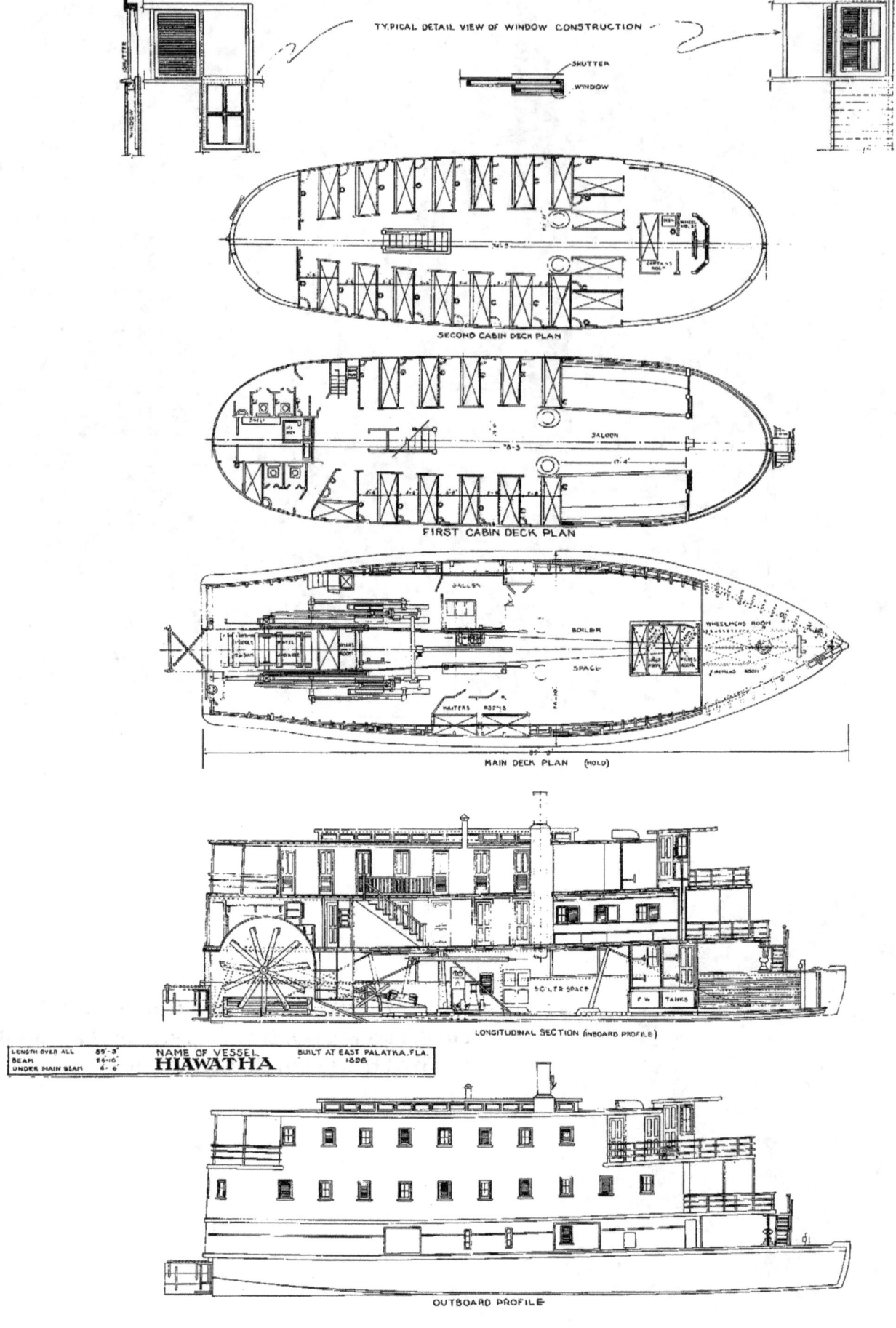

TYPICAL DETAIL VIEW OF WINDOW CONSTRUCTION

SHUTTER
WINDOW

SECOND CABIN DECK PLAN

FIRST CABIN DECK PLAN

MAIN DECK PLAN (HOLD)

LONGITUDINAL SECTION (INBOARD PROFILE)

LENGTH OVER ALL	89'-3"	NAME OF VESSEL	BUILT AT EAST PALATKA, FLA.
BEAM	24'-0"	HIAWATHA	1898
UNDER MAIN BEAM	4'-0"		

OUTBOARD PROFILE

Captain Howard and the William Howard

Following is an excerpt (slightly edited) that Captain J. Hatten Howard, II wrote of his experiences on the WILLIAM HOWARD when she traversed the Ocklawaha River. Part of it was reprinted by the Lake County Historical Society many years ago. It originally appeared in the January, 1942 issue of *Motor Boating* magazine.

****

"THAT crash would have jolted a dreadnaught. It jarred every plank in the sturdy Florida river steamer, WILLIAM HOWARD. Instinctively I pulled the bell cord, signalling Stop. The action was unnecessary for even as the bell jangled, the 100 horsepower engine cracked, groaned and ceased to turn.

"Shore was less than a pebble's toss away on either side. All about us huge cypress trees stretched out their gaunt, moss-bearded arms. I designated a tree that would be easy to tie to, ordered Old Rail, the ancient, barefooted negro quartermaster, to head the boat for it, and then I hurried aft to find the reason for the terrific crashing and banging that still continued.

"Jim Kellix, the gray-headed negro engineer, a battered pipe in his mouth, a mammoth wrench in his hand, was gazing goggle-eyed at the wheelbox, that was behaving like a Mexican jumping bean. Some gigantic force inside it was wrenching and straining. A half dozen negro roustabouts stood nearby, jaws agape. Excited passengers clustered on the upper deck, now gazing at the wheelbox, now anxiously looking aloft to see if any serpent was preparing to drop from the lush, green branches overhead.

"'Cap'n, we done pick up Oscar!' one of the negroes exclaimed.

"He sho nuf makes a snug fit in dat wheelbox and he doan like it nohow," laughed a tall negro, white teeth gleaming.

"If we had picked up Oscar we had something on our hands. He was the largest alligator on the Ocklawaha River. Quickly my eyes scanned the shore. Yes, there was Oscar's pet log on which he invariably sunned himself—but there was no Oscar. Another series of crashing thuds made it evident where he was.

"Hawsers were run out to the thick, tall cypress trees. Then the crew, armed with pinchbars, began prying the paddlebox apart. As boards were removed Oscar's ugly tail came through the gap swinging like a huge pendulum. It was lassoed and snubbed fast. As other parts of him appeared they were quickly roped, until Oscar was bound up like an Egyptian mummy. His jaws were tied so close he couldn't have munched a marshmallow. Then he was removed bodily from the paddlebox, and the whole twelve feet of him laid out on the deck.

"Oscar had stopped the paddlewheel, but the wheel had not stopped Oscar. It hadn't even raised a blister, and hogtied as he was, he was still rarin' to go. I was glad Oscar had not been flattened out like a peppermint for he was a most accommodating 'gator. He was always in the same place, so skippers of Ocklawaha River steamers could announce to their passengers that they would see a 'gator around a certain bend—and they were seldom wrong. Oscar aimed to please.

"When a steamer passed, most 'gators would slither into the water and disappear. But not Oscar. He was a showoff. As the vessel drew abeam, he would plunge into the cool, greenish liquid with a splash, and make a long, graceful glide directly under the boat. In the crystal clear water the passengers would catch his every move, and they would line the rail uttering little gasps of oh-h-h-h-s and ah-h-h-h-s. Appearing on the opposite side, he would lie like a black log in the water, legs slowly moving, eyes protruding, and watch with keen enjoyment the excitement he had caused.

"But this day Oscar's timing was off. The big wheel sucked him up. We gave him a free ride to Silver Springs. There for more than a year he had the run of a pen and was admired by thousands of tourists. One day heavy rains fell. The river rose so high Oscar could get out of his pen without a stepladder. When morning came he had gone.

"A few days later the WILLIAM HOWARD came puffing up the river. There was Oscar on his favorite log. Once again there was a splash and the long, easy glide. Probably Oscar still waits on the same log, disconsolate now because no more steamers appear. Railroads and improved highways have driven from Florida rivers most of the picturesque old passenger boats. The beautiful Ocklawaha River is deserted. No steamers ply its water. Warehouses and docks have rotted and blended in with the forest. Frogs peep undisturbed and the cries of wildcats carom off the water. . . .

"When I think of the Ocklawaha River days, it seems I can still hear the negroes strumming on their guitars, and singing in the moonlight as the boat moved swiftly down the dark, tree-lined corridor of the river. The Ocklawaha, rapid and deep, except for a few bars, winds north and east and connects with the St. Johns River at Welaka. To me it has always seemed the most beautiful river in the state. Unlike the many muddy rivers in the South, it is as transparent as glass, and looking down from a steamer's deck one can see trout and bass darting about, and watch the countless variety of submarine plants slowly bend and sway. But the river's bed might have been laid out by an acrobat with a nightmare. It doubles and bends, twists and turns, makes loops and twirls. In fact, it goes through about every contortion except handsprings and somersaults. The bends actually take up more than half the river's length. The steamer I operated ran from Silver Springs to Palatka, which is north of Welaka on the St. Johns. It is only fifty miles from Silver Springs to Palatka in a pigeon's flight, but 125 miles via the Ocklawaha River.

"I was just a youngster when father started his own steamer on the Ocklawaha. His first boat was a little 49-foot, canopy-topped, wood-burner called the SOPHIE HOWARD. Then he built the MARY HOWARD, a 54-footer. Both boats were propeller driven, but those wheels caused heaps of grief when they tangled with water hyacinths. To eliminate this trouble, father had the WILLIAM HOWARD built. She was a sternwheeler, 85 feet long.

"This latter boat was considered a river palace. She was white with three decks and, though primarily a freighter, she had accommodations for eighteen passengers. The crew numbered eleven, all happy-go-lucky negroes. They bunked in the fo'c's'le, had their plates heaped with food at the galley door, and lounged on the freight deck to eat.

"My father's death occurred soon after I was graduated from the Georgia School of Technology. I had always been susceptible to the lure of boats, so I bought the WILLIAM HOWARD from the estate and continued her in the Silver Springs-Palatka run.

"It took two days to make the northbound, downstream trip to Palatka, and three days for the upstream journey. During all that time the eyes of the passengers fairly popped, trying to drink in the beauty of that swift, swampy river with its luxuriant vegetation. The trees linked their branches overhead like clasped hands, making a veritable covered hallway of rich, green foliage. White herns and egrets polka-dotted the river banks. Cranes stood about solemnly on stiltlike legs. Alligators, large and small, slept on the reedy shores. Water moccasins, thick as a man's neck, and long, slim watersnakes, idled on partly submerged logs, raising their heads as the boat passed and flicking out long, needlelike tongues.

"The transportation charge was the same for either the two- or three-day trip. It was $5.00 a person, and that included berth and meals. The menu would make a gourmand grin. The cook was Joe Crowell, a shufflin', singin' old negro, who was supposed to keep his shoes on, but didn't always do it. But he sported a white chef's hat and white apron, and when it came to concocting tasty viands he had the touch of a master.

"For breakfast the main dish was always bass that were practically tossed from the river to the frying pan. Little Mack, a diminutive negro deckhand, could hurl a three-pronged gaff with the speed of a striking rattler. Just before breakfast he would stand at the boat's bow, eyes scanning the dark depths of the water, gaff poised for a throw. Suddenly Little Mack's arm would snap down and the gaff would shoot into the river. When pulled back, a bass was always wriggling on the barbed prongs. By the time the passengers entered the dining room there would be a mess of fat, luscious bass browning in the pan.

"At dinner and supper the meat course would usually be wild turkey, chicken, venison or quail. Such delicacies were really the cheapest food to serve, for many stops were made, and at all docks farmers and hunters waited with birds and game to sell. Turkey gobblers could be bought for $1.00 apiece, turkey hens for 75 cents. Venison cost only a few cents a pound. Spring chicken sold for ten cents apiece, mature birds for 25 cents. Eggs were seven cents a dozen. I always bought all the eggs offered and disposed of them at the trip's end for a profit of two cents a dozen. Often we would arrive at Palatka with many thousand eggs aboard.

"Our bill of fare included all kinds of fresh vegetables, oranges and grapefruit just off the trees. If we happened to pass a succulent looking cabbage palm I would put the boat against the bank long enough for a crew member to cut its green, tender tip. Cabbage palm was a great treat for the Northerners. Old Joe would boil part of it with cornbeef, and the remainder he would turn into coleslaw.

"There were thrills aplenty on a river trip. Occasionally a big snake would drop slithering to the deck from the overhanging branches. With shrieks and screams the passengers would scatter like shrapnel. But the snake always seemed as eager to leave the boat as we were to have it go. It would dart through the rail and hit the water with a splash.

"Aside from the WILLIAM HOWARD, there were four other steamers on the river. These belonged to the Hart Line. . . . The river was too narrow for boats to pass, its average width being only about forty feet. In one place the trunks of two huge cypress trees, on opposite sides of the river, had been gouged out so the guardrails of steamers could slip through. Downbound boats had the right of way. When the blast of a downbounder echoed through the forest the upbound boat scuttled for some lagoon or river mouth, and laid low until the way was clear. There was usually ample time for such a maneuver, for though the warning whistle boomed out from just a few rods away through the forest, the vessels were probably miles apart as the river ran.

"The steamers would come down awhizzing. It was a trick to make the turns, for some of them were so sharp even a water moccasin would have to watch its wiggle. At these hairpin curves the procedure was this: The pilot would jam the steamer's bow hard on the point. The swift current, catching the vessel's stern, would slew it around. At the proper instant the engine roared in reverse, freeing the bow; and then the bells clanged for full speed ahead. Curve after curve was negotiated in this manner. By the time the passengers reached Palatka, they felt as though they had been jiggled in a cocktail shaker. When the steamer slewed around the curves, she often raked the trees on the opposite bank. In the process some of the boats had holes punched through them. To avoid this the WILLIAM HOWARD was sheathed bow and stern—and most of her length—in thick, live oak planks. She was so stout she could butt the trees and only the trees would suffer.

"In order to complete the upstream journey in three days and the downtrip in two, it was necessary to run late at night. The illumination for night running was provided by burning fat pine fagots. There was an iron pan, four feet square and eight inches deep, on top of the pilot house. This was filled with water, and in the water there was a smaller pan in which the fire was built. A negro kept the blaze roaring, and its flickering red light on trees and branches made navigation possible.

"Often ahead there would be twin, pinpoint glows on the water as a 'gator faced about inquisitively and eyed the boat. In the ebony shore blackness the eyes of wildcats, 'possum and foxes would gleam greenishly. Small Florida deer stood in full view of the shore, fascinated by the brilliant fire. When ten or eleven o'clock came we would call it a day, and if no dock was near, we would tie to some handy tree. The boat would rest in the jungle darkness, while the moon, peeping through the crossed branches, reflected in the river like a china plate. Strange night animals would scream, and there would be the mournful hooting of great swamp owls. Before turning in, the passengers often had songfests, and Suwanee River never sounded more beautiful than when it came from a mixed medley of voices in that wild and romantic setting. I made so many trips on the Ocklawaha that I could tell our position by trees and branches. One trip we had a new pilot aboard.

I walked to the upper deck after breakfast and was puzzled. None of the trees looked familiar.

"'Mr. Olmstead,' I queried, 'what river are we in?'

"He looked at me quizzically. 'The Ocklawaha,' he drawled, 'or I'll eat a lizard.'

"'Then you better start catching one,' I retorted with a grin.

"He looked dumbfounded as I signalled for reverse. We backed for ten minutes before we were where we belonged. Skilled though he was, Mr. Olmstead had turned the boat into one of the Ocklawaha's many tributaries.

"The river was a veritable hotbed for gorgeous, purple water hyacinths. A stream of the floating flowers, fifteen or twenty feet wide, was almost constantly disgorging into the St. Johns. Our big stern-wheeler could plough through the tangled plants, but often hyacinth-jams occurred. Sometimes a tree would fall, obstructing the river. If a steamer appeared soon, she would nose up to the tree, and the crew would disembark and chop it away. But if no boat came along for a day or two, a downbound vessel might find the river a mass of flowers a mile or two back from the obstruction. Such a jam would be impossible to punch through. In an emergency of this nature our faithful old wheelman, Rail, would put on hip boots and flounder through the swampy, snake-infested jungle until he located the cause of the stoppage. With a axe he would chop it away.

"I have seen hyacinths packed so solid a person could lay a board on them and walk on it. Occasionally during a jam, they would become massed so tight they would not start moving after the cause was removed. Then the crew members would place planks on the hyacinths and saw them out in blocks like cakes of ice.

"Hyacinths are not as great a nuisance to navigation as they once were, for the U.S. Engineers, with boats that cut through them like lawnmowers, are waging a relentless hyacinth war. Before this was started I have seen the St. Johns River, in places where it is a mile wide, just one mass from shore to shore, of these beautiful, purple, pestiferous flowers.

"Today you can get in your car at Palatka, step on the accelerator, and z-o-o-m, you're in Silver Springs in an hour. But you have missed all the sights and pleasures of the old days. On the WILLIAM HOWARD, the passengers quickly got acquainted. It was like a big houseparty. The Hart Line boats were faster, with better accommodations, but many persons preferred to ride on the HOWARD, for being a freighter, she made frequent stops at the little wisps of river settlements. While we loaded and unloaded, the passengers hobnobbed with the natives, picked jungle flowers, or filled baskets with delicious, tropical fruit. A blast of the whistle would bring them scurrying to the dock like a covey of partridges.

"I owned an orange grove at Delk's Bluff. It was six miles from Grahamville to the Bluff by water, but less than two miles by trail through the grove. At Grahamville all passengers able to hobble would disembark, and I would conduct them through the grove, meeting the boat at the Delk's' Bluff dock. Passengers could take all the fruit they could eat or carry away. Old Rail, the negro quartermaster, would be in charge of the boat for the six mile run. During that brief journey he was the world's proudest darkey.

"We made one round trip a week, leaving Silver Springs on Monday and returning Saturday. On each run there were at least seventeen stops. Going downstream, regular ports of call north of Silver Springs were Delk's Bluff, Grahamville, Conner, Durisoe's Landing, Gore's Landing, Sunday Bluff, Eureka, Dexter, Tobacco Patch, Forty Foot Bluff, Orange Springs, Jordan's Landing, Fort Brook, Sims' Landing, Cedar Landing, Riverside and Davenport. The HOWARD was a wood burner and at every dock cord wood would be stacked in high, fragrant piles. We could load only four cords at a time, and it took eighteen cords for a round trip. Wood cost $2.00 a cord.

"Some of the river ports were up-and-coming places. Take Eureka as an example. It had three big docks with large warehouses at each one. There was a church and several stores. Two years ago I passed the site in a yacht, and it looked as though jungle growths had swept over everything. Trees, forty feet high, stood like tombstones to mark the place where the warehouses had once been.

"Grahamville, near Silver Springs, was the place where I was born. The territory was just a tangled forest when my father purchased land and moved there in 1885. He named the place for John Graham, an old friend who lived in the vicinity, and who became the town's first postmaster. Father put up a cotton gin, a grist mill, a saw mill, and he opened a general store that sold everything from plow shares to ladies' hats.

"The backwoods dwellers, who sat about on the store cracker barrels, would make perfect story characters. The one who stands out clearest in my mind was an old hunter and trapper who wore a fur cap winter and summer, invariably had a wad of tobacco bunched in his cheek, and was never without his ancient, muzzle-loading rifle. He even placed it across his lap when he sat in the store. This old patriarch had been snake-bitten, no one knew how many times, and he could drawl out jungle tales that would make us kids lie awake nights and shiver. In the minds of the youngsters of Grahamville, Daniel Boone was a piker compared to Jungle Jake.

"The house I was born in was known as a two-pen log cabin. That meant two rooms with a small passage between. The most important thing about the cabin was the huge fireplace, made from a mixture of dirt and sticks. All cooking was done in the fireplace. In it was a rack on which the pots were hung. Two years after I was born, father built an eleven-room mansion that was the show place of the forest country. It had eleven fireplaces and was piped for gas-but we never got the gas. Living in the outlands, I never went to school a day in my life. My grandmother was my tutor. She was so proficient that at Georgia Tech I surprised the faculty by graduating with second honors. Grahamville is in the heart of the country described in *The Yearling*. In fact, it is mentioned in that 'popular' novel. Now an isolated turpentine camp is all that is left of my old home town.

"River trade prospered until the Ocklawaha Valley Railroad was built. This road was put in by the E. P. Rantz Lumber Company, and it connected Palatka with Silver Springs. It wrote finis for the steamboats, and in time the highways and motor trucks spelled doom for it. That railroad, like the steamer docks, has long been buried deep in jungle foliage.

"The Ocklawaha River still flows seaward in all its beauty. Occasionally some yachtsman, with a yen for exploration, makes the run from the St. Johns to Silver Springs. A friend of mine came down the river in a canoe last year, and he described it as the wildest country he had ever been in. During the four-day trip he saw one hunter, but no other signs of civilization . . ."

Above, Captain Howard's propeller craft MARY HOWARD, OKAHUMKEE at right rear. *Below,* circa late 1870s Palatka scene—at left, LOLLIE BOY, FORRESTER (middle) and OCKLAWAHA at right. The latter two vessels ran on the Ocklawaha River.

The WILLIAM HOWARD built in 1902. *Left,* with a heavy load of freight. *Below,* tied up at Delk's Bluff, heading downstream (popular post card of the time).

The 1902 WILLIAM HOWARD. *Above,* at Silver Springs. *Right,* at Eureka, heading downstream. Recessed sternwheel is running. Closure doors are open as paddlewheel is being especially run for this photo which was made into a post card.

Above, The WILLIAM HOWARD, now named TOURIST, in a fake night view. The day photo shown *below* has been retouched to make the night time view, which was a popular post card of its time.

The Hart Line countered the Carmichael's daylight line for a short spell with its day launch BILLOW. Shown here circa 1920 as sunk and then *(below)* salvaged by the Merrill Stevens Corporation of Jacksonville.

One of the Silver Springs Daylight Line passenger boats the "Silver Springs" on one of its many excursions.

Two of the Mills Line vessels of the 1910s. *Above,* HEL-KAT, named after Everett Mills' daughters, Helen and Kate. *Below,* SHARP SHOOTER #2.

END OF THE LINE! *Left,* OKAHUMKEE tied up in the St. Johns River at Hart's Point, East Palatka, 1930s. *Below,* HIAWATHA, also at Hart's Point.

Part 2

Around the Next Bend

"AROUND THE NEXT BEND"
THE OCKLAWAHA RIVER

We will start our journey down the Ocklawaha River at Starkes Ferry Bridge at Highway 42, which is north of Lake Griffin, one of the lakes that make up the headwaters of the Ocklawaha River.

Just north of the Starkes Ferry Bridge we will enter the canal that was dug to drain the area west of the river to make it suitable for farming and cattle grazing. Recently, the St. Johns Water Management has attempted to divert the flow of the water back to the old river bed.

The distance from Starkes to the Moss Bluff lock is about 7 ½ miles. The lock and dam were built in 1925-1926, as a hydro plant to produce electric power. The power plant is no longer in service. The lock and dam were built to control the water level in Lake Harris and Lake Griffin. The bridge at Moss Bluff is just downstream from the lock and dam.

We continue downstream about 6 ½ miles to the Kyle-Young Canal. The canal was dug to drain the property between the canal and the river. With the dredge they had, they could only dig the canal to a shallow depth that would not accommodate boat traffic. They had messed up the canal and the river to the point where boats could not use them. The U.S. Army Corps of Engineers had to come in and dig the canal to a depth suitable for boat traffic. This was completed in 1913. The ownership of the Ocklawaha Muck Farms has changed several times since then.

We enter back into the Ocklawaha River about 1 mile downstream from the canal. This is the vicinity of the old Heather Island Ferry and Heather Island Landing. The area to the southwest of the river is known as Heather Island. In 1899, Mr. Charles Hulburd purchased a large part of the island and built a large southern style mansion on the property. He was very wealthy and used the mansion to entertain the employees of his company and his friends.

About 3 miles downstream from Heather Island Landing we come to the Sharpes Ferry Bridge where Highway 314 crosses the river. Although the ferry site is no longer in use, the original bridge has recently been replaced with a modern bridge.

About 2 ½ miles downstream from Sharpes Ferry Bridge is the junction of the Ocklawaha River and Silver River. It is a sight to behold where the dark waters of the Ocklawaha and the clear waters of the Silver River meet.

The Native American meaning of Ocklawaha is "dark crooked water."

"AROUND THE NEXT BEND"
FLORIDA'S SILVER SPRINGS - IN THE EARLY DAYS

We begin the next segment of our journey down the Ocklawaha River at Florida's Silver Springs, which is about 5 miles east of Ocala.

Silver Springs is truly one of nature's greatest accomplishments. Many people have tried to describe the beauties of the springs, and all have failed to capture the beauty with words. You have to see it to believe and appreciate it.

You can take a trip on one of the "Glass Bottom" boats and view the many springs and attractions in and around the headwaters of Silver Springs, then take the "Jungle Cruise" boats to see the Silver River wonderland with all its tropical foliage and wildlife, including the Rhesus monkeys. This will be a trip you will never forget!

In the 1930s and early-1940s you could visit Silver Springs with no charge for admission. You could buy a ticket to go on one of the Glass Bottom boats or one of the Jungle Cruise boats. There were souvenir and antique shops, and you could get ice cream and cold drinks from the vendors. You could also take a swim in the cool, 72 degree, clear waters of the springs free of charge.

The owners of Silver Springs would hold an annual Easter Sunrise Service each year at the head of the springs. The boat "Sunbeam" located at the Highway 40 Bridge, would take passengers up the Silver River to attend the Sunrise Services. They would also hold an Easter Egg Hunt for all the children in the area.

Gigging at Silver Springs.

Visiting Ladies Parlor at Silver Springs.

Ladies in their bonnets out rowing on Silver Springs.

Seeing Silver Springs through glass bottomed rowboat.

RIVERBOATS AT SILVER SPRINGS

The Okeehumkee at the head of the springs.

Riverboat at the head of the springs shot from the top of the rail station.

The Okeehumkee at the head of the Silver Springs rail station with early glass bottom boat.

The Okeehumkee at the head of the springs.

Two riverboats moored downstream on the Silver River.

VIEWS OF LIFE AT SILVER SPRINGS

Tourists enjoying the beauty of Silver Springs.

Riverboat leaving the springs on the Silver River.

Early glass bottom boat at the boat house.

Rowboats located at the springs boat house.

Tourists enjoying a tour of Silver Springs with riverboat in the background.

THE LEGEND OF THE BRIDAL CHAMBER
at SILVER SPRINGS

This legend was written many years ago by the gifted hand of an unknown author and has been passed down through the ages. Aunt Lucilla, often called "Scilla," was a well-known native of Ocala and frequented Silver Springs during the early years of the riverboats.

Near Florida's celebrated Silver Springs lives an old Negro woman, known to the entire surrounding country as "Aunt Scilla." Her claim to being 110 years old is borne out by her appearance. Her face is wrinkled and worn, with wiry, white hair peeking out from under the bandanna on her head, and her ancient black face is intensified by a heavy crop of snow-white beard. Many of the oldest citizens of Ocala still remember Aunt Scilla hobbling about Silver Springs leaning upon her short, thick staff, and only a few of them would talk about the tragedy thrust upon poor Aunt Scilla in those early days.

Close to Silver Springs, in the neighboring community of Ocala, stood a splendid old mansion, owned by Capt. Harding Douglass, a South Carolinian of considerable wealth. His only child, Claire Douglas, was a son who had inherited his mother's beauty as well as her tender, shrinking nature. Like his mother, he was a slave to the old man's iron will.

Also in the little city of Ocala lived Bernice Mayo, a blonde beauty of Virginia ancestry. She was a true child of the "Land of Flowers," passionate and impulsive. Her eyes were blue and as clear as the waters of Lake Munroe, beside which she had spent her childhood in the fair City of Sanford. Bernice won the heart of Claire Douglass the first time he saw her. Her golden hair the color of sunshine and her tropical nature captured his heart. For six months Bernice Mayo and Claire Douglass were constant companions, and Sliver Springs was their favorite spot to explore the wonders of nature.

At the Springs, Bernice never seemed to tire of going into the depths of the subterranean world. "If I were a mermaid, Claire," she would say, "and lived in the crystal cavern, I would sit on the rock ledge and comb my golden hair with a shell. I would wander among the palmettos and moss of the springs, and if your boat should come drifting by, and you were to see me in the water beneath, would you love me enough to plunge to the depths beneath to woo me?" Then, as they drifted over the transparent mirror of water, Claire would stop her merry chatter with his kisses and pledge to her his eternal love. For these young lovers, nothing intensified their love greater than the waters and woodlands of Silver Springs.

But there came a fatal day destined to separate them. On that day Claire Douglass declared to his father his love for the beautiful, but penniless, Bernice Mayo, and his determination to make her his wife. Seething beneath a calm exterior, his father vowed it should never be and secretly planned their separation. Claire Douglass was speedily dispatched abroad on important business for his father.

When Bernice learned the truth, her proud, delicate nature lay crushed and bleeding beneath the cruel blow of their separation. Vainly she strove to rally, but all life seemed empty and hopeless. A year dragged wearily by, and the waters and woodlands frequented by merry Bernice Mayo knew her no more. She grew paler and thinner every day. She became as fragile as the white blossoms of her well-loved springs. The little chain of gold that Claire had locked on her arm would have slipped across the wasted, transparent hand, but for the ribbon that held its links.

One day (her last upon earth) the girl, by dint of desperate energy, crept to Silver Springs. Even Aunt Scilla was unprepared for the white, emaciated little creature who tottered through her cabin door and fell fainting in her arms. Consciousness soon returned, but it was apparent even to the old black woman that death had set its gray, unmistakable seal upon the young face.

"Aunt Scilla," gasped the girl, "I have come to you to die, and you must obey my last request. By tonight's sunset I

Aged "Aunt Lucilla" termed "Scilla", was renowned for relating the Legend of the Bridal Chamber (a tale of a lovers' suicide pact) at Silver Springs.

shall be in Heaven. This separation from the man I love has been my death, but we will be reunited. I have asked God, and He has heard me. But you, Aunt Scilla, you must obey my request. You love me; you will do as I ask. Tonight when the moon comes out, row my body to Boiling Springs and bury me there. You know the spot; make no mistake. Do this, and God will attend to the rest."

"Good Lord A'mighty, chile, you think Aunt Scilla gonna tote dat body off in the lonesome night?" ask the old woman, her very teeth chattering with superstitious fear. The girl realized the risk of her plan being thwarted, and raising herself to a sitting posture she seized the old woman's hands and fixed her dying eyes full on her face.

"Aunt Scilla," she gasped, "I am a dying woman, and I am very near to God. I have talked with Him, and He has answered me. My will has been crushed in life; I swear it shall not be in death. Before twenty-four hours pass, Claire Douglass shall join me in the crystal cavern of Silver Springs. If you do not grant my request every spirit of evil will surround you. You will grow palsied, blind, and deaf… deaf to every sound but the ghosts of the dead, which shall pursue you by day and haunt you by night. Do you swear to obey my dying request, or will you refuse me, and reap the prophecy of a dying woman, which shall rest upon your cowardly head for refusing to obey God's will?"

The old woman was shaking like an aspen. Her eyes protruded with fear, and great beads of perspiration rolled down her cheeks. The strength of the dying girl's will had prevailed, and the old woman answered, "I Promises, honey. I promises."

It was a solemn sight that night, witnessed only by God and nature: the boat drifting down Silver Springs in the moonlight, bearing its two strange occupants… one bent, old, grotesque woman; one so silent, so white, so pathetic, in her dead loveliness. Not a leaf was stirring, not a sound to be heard except for the splash, splash of the old woman's oars, as her boat, with its strange, beautiful burden, drifted over the curiously transparent water.

The boat glided silently until it reached Boiling Springs, then veered about and stood still. Gently and easily, as if it had been a babe, the old woman lifted the little body. Something of her fear had departed in the placid smile of the dead girl's face. Tears rolled down her dusky face as she bent forward in obedience to the girl's curious request. For a moment the body rocked to and fro on the bottom of the water, upon which its happiest moments had been spent. The dead face smiled, and the wealth of hair gleamed in the moonlight like a sheen of gold. Every pebble was visible in the depths below. Suddenly, as if by magic, the body began sinking. The boiling of the spring had ceased, showing a peculiar little fissure in the rock from whence all the strange body of water came. The fissure slowly divided,

received the dead body and closed again, shutting every vestige of it from view.

"Lord A'mighty, dat chile's an angel sho' nuff. She mus' done talked to de Lawd; she knowed how all dat gonna be," muttered the old woman as she rowed back to her cabin in the moonlight. A mockingbird on the opposite shore sent forth a flood of silvery melody. "Hear dat now," muttered Aunt Scilla; "dat bird done gone sendin' forth de weddin' song of de bridegroom. Come on, Claire Douglass, yo' little bride's awaitin'."

The day following the death of Bernice Mayo was one never to be forgotten by the citizens of Ocala. Claire Douglass had just returned after a year's absence. He found his beautiful cousin (whom his father desired to become his wife) a guest at the home of his parents.

"Claire," said his father as they lingered over the breakfast table, "I have a fine new skiff at Silver Springs, and I wish you to take your cousin for a row this morning; and, by the permission of you young people, I shall make one of your party."

"Delightful, uncle!" cried the girl; and Claire, turning a trifle pale at the thought of returning to the spot where all that had given color to his life had transpired, could only acquiesce…

Claire Douglass looked unusually handsome as the party drifted down Silver Springs in the April sunshine, but there was a curious pallor on his face, and the uncle and niece were left to carry all the conversation. (What a contrast the blooming girl in the April sunshine bore to the one in the solemn moonlight, who had drifted over the same water the evening before!) As the skiff neared Boiling Springs the party noted a little boat hovering over it. The boat was rowed by Aunt Silly, and its other occupant was an old woman, whose eyes were swollen and weeping. The skiff paused beside the little rowboat, and the occupants of each gazed into the curious, transparent depths below.

Suddenly the niece cried out, "Oh, see, that looks like a hand, a little human hand!" Plainer and more visible it grew, the little white hand with its gold chain locked about the slender wrist. "Ah, little hand," Claire Douglass thought. "I would know you among ten thousand hands!" His face was white as death, and he gasped as though choking. All were intent upon the scene below. Suddenly, the boiling of the water ceased, and out upon a rock in its transparent depths, lay Bernice Mayo, her golden hair floating on the sand, her dead face smiling placidly, as if at last a halo of peace had descended upon the tired spirit and broken heart. She had found rest.

With a wild cry Claire Douglass leaped overboard, diving deeper, ever deeper, until he caught in his arms the little figure of his dead love. Then once more the rock divided

A view down into the "Bridal Chamber" from 60 feet above the cavern.

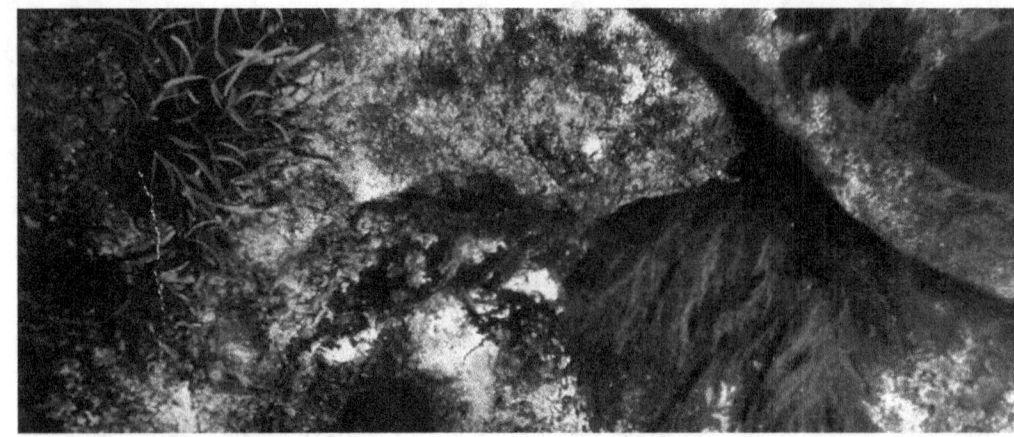

and closed, shutting from view forever the two lovers who lay locked in each other's embrace. And again the waters whirled and boiled in mad fury, as if to defy the puny will of him who would have separated what God had joined together.

By legend, the secret bridal chamber of Silver Springs has been made known to the world. As future visitors approach the part of the springs known as "Boiling Springs," they see the whirl of water beneath the perfectly placid surface, and the constant shower of tiny, pearl-like shells pouring forth from the fissure in the rock. Aunt Silly says they are the jewels that the angels gave Bernice upon her wedding morning when her lover joined her in their fairy palace in Silver Springs. There is also a curious flower growing in the springs – a flower with a leaf like a lily, and a blossom shaped like an orange blossom. Its peculiar waxy whiteness and yellow V-shaped petals are like Bernice Mayo's face and hair. Aunt Silly calls them "Bernice's Bridal Wreath." There is also a legend among the young people of Ocala that a woman presented with one of these blossoms will become a bride before the year's end.

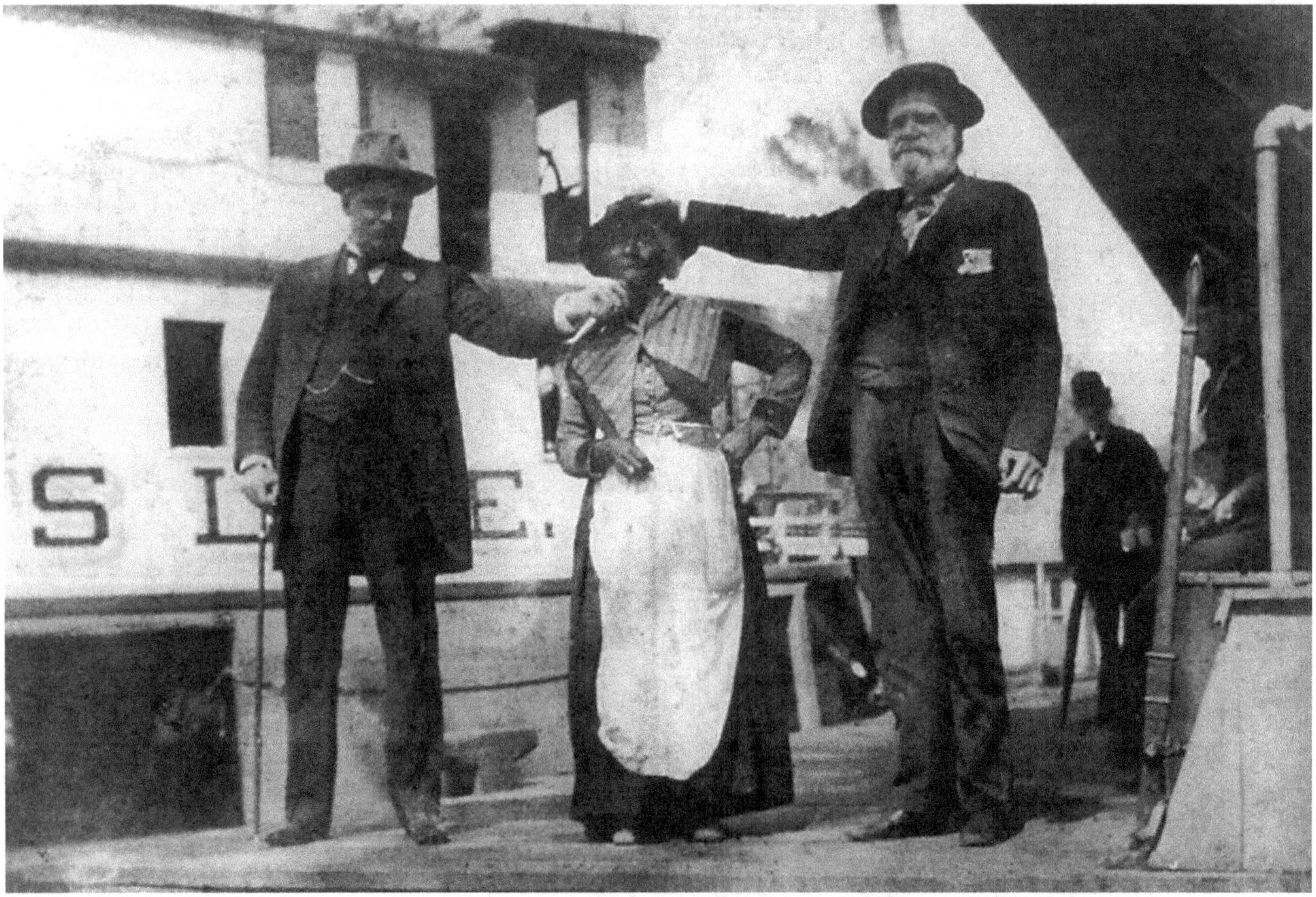

Captain Henry Gray, on right, poses with Aunt Scilla and an admirer.

THE "SILVER SPRINGS" DAYLIGHT LINE

**Head of Silver Springs.
Freight and Passenger Boats at Landing.**

The Silver Springs Daylight Line was owned by Mr. G. A. Carmichael. It consisted of three vessels, the "City of Ocala" built in 1912, and the "Silver Springs" built in 1915. Both were passenger boats. The third vessel was the "G. A. Carmichael," a freight boat. All three boats were built in Silver Springs.

The passenger boats would leave each morning from Silver Springs and Palatka and arrive that afternoon at the opposite landing. The passenger boat would travel between the two points several times during the week. The boats only traveled during daylight hours, thus the reason for the name Daylight Line.

The Mason family has lived and worked on the Ocklawaha River for five generations. The bond between the river and the family has grown stronger through the years. William Carl Mason was captain of the Daylight Line passenger boat "City of Ocala" that traveled between Silver Springs and Palatka. He was also captain of the "Joe Borden Glass Bottom Boats" in later years.

William Carl Mason, Captain, and L. G. Gallant, Engineer, of the "City of Ocala" passenger boat.

VIEWS OF LIFE AT SILVER SPRINGS

Swimming beach and dive tower at Silver Springs.

Newer glass bottom boats at the springs.

High dive tower with glass bottom boats in background.

Sightseers gazing at the thousands of fish below.

A bathing beauty spending time at Silver Springs.

For years this palm tree amazed many tourists.

SILVER SPRINGS JUNGLE CRUISE

Many visitors to Silver Springs enjoyed the Jungle Cruise Adventure.

In the 1930s two Jungle Cruise boats were put into operation at Silver Springs to take the tourists on a jungle cruise down the Silver River after they had taken a ride on the Glass Bottom boats.

Leland Mason was the captain of the "LEE. M," a Jungle Cruise boat that was named for him.

The captain would take the tourists down the Silver River for several miles pointing out the wildlife: deer; alligators; snakes; turtles; and all kinds of birds that lived along the banks of the river. One of the main attractions along the swamp was the Rhesus monkeys. The boat would turn around at Monkey Island and head back up the river to Silver Springs.

The monkeys were brought to the Silver Springs area in the 1930s. Some say they were brought here by the movie people when they were making the Tarzan movies. Others say they were brought here by the owners of Silver Springs as an additional tourist attraction. We don't know which version is correct; they served both purposes. The monkeys were put on Monkey Island where they were supposed to stay. No one told them to stay on the island, and they were soon up and down the swamp from Silver Springs to the junction of the Silver River and the Ocklawaha River. On each trip down the river, the captain would take oranges, apples, bananas, bread, and other things that monkeys like to eat and stop the boat and feed them. They soon got used to this and would meet the boat for a handout.

The Lee. M cruising on the Silver River.

Sometimes the monkeys would stray downstream to the junction of the Silver River and the Ocklawaha River. The captain would run the boat downriver to where they were. He would blow the boat whistle to get their attention. The monkeys knew he had food on the boat so they would follow him back up the river to Monkey Island where he would feed them.

Leland Mason was the Captain of the Lee. M Jungle Cruise boat which showcased the scenic river and the Rhesus monkeys.

SILVER RIVER and the OCKLAWAHA RIVER

The distance from the head of Silver Springs to the junction of the Ocklawaha River is nine miles by boat and five miles by car on Highway 40.

When steamboats were carrying freight and passengers up and down the river, there were ten landings between Silver Springs and the junction of the Silver River and the Ocklawaha River. Today, only one or two still show evidence of ever existing.

As we travel down Silver River, we marvel at how clear the water is. You can see the bottom of the river from bank to bank.

About 8 miles downriver we come to a canal on the north side of the river leading north to "RAY'S WAYSIDE PARK." The park has two boat ramps, a large pavilion, and a playground.

Where the two rivers join you can see the difference in how clear the water is between the Silver and the Ocklawaha Rivers. Sometimes, at the junction of the two rivers, you could see otters playing around and catching fish for their dinner. They are always fun to watch.

About half a mile downstream from the junction of the rivers, we come to the Highway 40 Bridge. This "skyway" bridge was built in the late 1960s and early 1970s to accommodate barge traffic on the Barge Canal that was to run from the St. Johns River across the state to the Gulf of Mexico. The canal was never completed, but we still have the bridge. This bridge replaced one of the old "swing" type bridges.

In the 1940s, Mr. Borden purchased the boat "SUNBEAM" and put it into operation carrying tourists up and down the Silver River. They also made trips down the Ocklawaha River to Eureka and returned. Mr. Borden also had a boat rental located at the Highway 40 Bridge and he rented boats to fishermen who were allowed to fish on the Ocklawaha River but not on the Silver River.

Clear water flowing upstream from the Silver River merging with the dark tannic water of the Ocklawaha.

JOE BORDEN GLASS BOTTOM BOATS

SHOWING FAMOUS SILVER SPRINGS

Cruise through 14 miles of jungle that is enjoyable any season of the year. The average daily flow of Silver Springs is 550,000,000 gallons at 72 degrees. Thus the valley is always ideally "air- conditioned."

New, modern glass bottom boats with restrooms, manned by white government-licensed operators, ensure your safety and comfort. People that know say that we give the best and finest trip for the money in the area.

By all means, bring a camera. You'll see the "locations" of many movies and newsreels…alligators sunning on sandy banks…myriads of turtles and fish… monkeys seeking handouts…jungle orchids, lilies, hyacinths, ferns…and an underwater

panorama that is a wonder to behold when viewed through a Joe Borden Glass Bottom Boat.

It's the most economical way, the most comfortable way, the nicest way to see famous Silver Springs, plus 14-mile scenic cruise over crystal-clear waters of Silver Springs River, from mouth to source.

Joe Borden Glass Bottom Boats docks are located on Florida Highway 40 at the Oklawaha River Bridge, 10 miles east of Ocala, Florida.

Above, an advertisement for Joe Borden Glass Bottom Boats in the late 1940s. *Below*, glass bottom boat on the Ocklawaha River. Joe Borden, Owner, and William Carl Mason, Captain.

GRAHAMVILLE LANDING and FERRY

We continue our journey downstream, north, from Highway 40 Bridge and Delks Bluff Landing for about 6 miles to Grahamville Landing and the Grahamville Ferry location. The Grahamville Ferry no longer exists.

Just upstream from the landing is the site where a "turpentine" still was located in the 1920s and 1930s.

The barrels of turpentine would be picked up by steamboats and taken to Jacksonville. The distilling of the rosin was discontinued in the early 1920s when trucks put the boats out of business. This is when the rosin began being shipped to Jacksonville by trucks.

There is a story about Dr. Lisk who lived at Conner. He drove a horse and buggy to treat patients living on both sides of the river. One morning before daylight he was returning home after treating a patient at Burbank on the west side of the river, and he must have fallen asleep in the buggy. When the horse arrived at the ferry landing, he stopped because the ferry was on the east side of the river. Dr. Lisk woke up and thinking the horse had stopped before he got to the ferry landing, gave the horse a tap with his whip and the horse lunged forward into the river. Both Dr. Lisk and the horse drowned in the river. A sad but true story.

The settlers on the east side of the river used the ferry to cross the river and travel by horse and wagons to Silver Springs and Ocala for supplies and maybe to sell a little "moonshine" whiskey.

Mr. John Conner Graham came to this area in 1848 and settled in the area that is known as the Conner-Grahamville area. Both Conner and Grahamville were named for Mr. Graham.

Downstream, about half a mile from Grahamville Landing, we come to Turkey Creek and Turkey Landing. Turkey Creek used to be a good place to catch all kinds of fish. Turkey Landing was used by fisherman to launch their boats. It is no longer in service and is closed to the public today.

CONNER LANDING and the RANDALL HOME

About half a mile downstream from Turkey Creek, we arrive at Conner Landing. Conner Landing was one of the most popular landings on the river for the steamboats in the 1800s and gas powered boats during the early 1900s.

Conner Landing was in use from the 1800s to the early 1900s. The Pat Randall Hotel was just up the hill from the landing. The hotel was a general store and post office at first. The top part of the building was added later to create a hotel. The landing was popular with the tourists because it was a place they could pick oranges and visit with the settlers in the area.

Conner Landing has been used and enjoyed by many families since the early 1900s. Henry Mason, Jr. and his family moved from Mason Mill Creek to Conner in 1905. He used the landing for his boating operation for many years.

In the 1930s, Edward Mason bought one of the older Glass Bottom boats from the owner of Silver Springs and moved it to Conner Landing. He used it as a houseboat and as a "base of operations" for his occupation, which was catching snakes and frogs, and killing alligators for their hides. That was the way he made his living. The boat he used as a houseboat is now at the Silver River Museum. In the 1950s, he had clientele built up in the Ocala area. He would make a trip to Silver Springs and Ocala every two or three weeks to sell what he had caught or killed. The first stop would be Ross Allen's Reptile Institute in Silver Springs to sell his snakes and turtles. He would sell the frog legs to a restaurant at Silver Springs. Then he would sell the alligator hides to a man on the west side of Ocala.

Conner Landing was once the place to go and enjoy fishing, swimming, boating, picnics, and just being on the river. Now, when coming down the river by boat, you cannot even tell when you get to the old landing. It is covered with brush and trees, and there is no way to get to the landing from the hill. "Greenway Park," a government agency which owns the land to the river's edge, has control of the area.

The William Howard stops at Conner Landing where tourists could admire its beauty.

The William Howard riverboat on the Ocklawaha River.

The citrus grove and flowing well were popular with the tourists at Conner Landing. The Hiawatha is in the background.

RANDALL HOME BURNS in the LATE 1920s

RANDALL HOME BY THE OCKLAWAHA

For Many Years a Landmark for Boats and a Haven for Friends, Was Destroyed Thursday by Fire.

Many people of Marion County, particularly those who live by and journey on the Oklawaha River, well know the historic Randall home at Conner, prominent on the high hill overlooking the river and surrounded by a fine orange grove, from which thousands of tourists have picked fruit. All these will hear with regret that this home was burned Thursday. The house was entirely destroyed by the fire which started in the second story and was not discovered until too late to save the place. Only a few things in the house were saved. There was a small amount of insurance on the house, but the damage which the fire did to the surrounding grove will not be covered.

Since the death of Mr. Pat Randall, the builder and well known owner, his son, Mr. George Randall, and wife have been making the house their home. Their friends will sincerely regret to hear of their loss.

The Randall home burned in the late 1920s and was never rebuilt. The above article is from a local newspaper of the time period.

TO THE "BLUFF" And The OLD "POLE" HOUSE

The Bluff is about 500 feet downstream, north, of Conner Landing. The "Bluff" is a hill about 25 feet high at a bend in the river.

In the 1930s, it was not unusual to see a "pole" house built along the river. There was one built right on the "Bluff" at Conner Landing. The house was framed with cypress poles cut from the cypress ponds. The outside of the house was sided in tin that looked like brick. There is no picture available, but there is a drawing of the house shown. It was about 24 feet wide and 50 feet long. There was a living room with a tin heater for the winter, a kitchen with a wood stove for cooking and heat. Three bedrooms were on the back of the house, and the "outhouse" was down the hill and only used as needed during the winter days.

Drinking water was carried by buckets from the "flowing" well at Conner Landing, up the hill to the house. Water for bathing was also carried by buckets from the river to the house. Both bathing and swimming were done down at the river. In the summer the water was a cool 72 degrees and a warm 72 degrees in the winter. The washing of clothes took place down at the river. Usually, there would be an iron pot for boiling the clothes, two wash tubs, one for washing and one for rinsing the clothes, and a washboard for scrubbing them clean. Once the clothes were clean, they would be carried up the hill to the house and hung on a line to dry. That was a typical "wash day" in the 1930s.

The house wasn't much compared to today's standards, but it was home. There weren't any electric lights in the house; kerosene lamps were used instead. In the winter blankets and quilts were piled high on the beds to keep everyone warm.

In 1946, the family who lived in the "pole" house moved to a piece of land on Conner Road. Because materials were hard to come by after the war, the owner bought an old building in Ocala, tore it down, and used the lumber and nails to build a new house. It had electric lights, a well and pump for running water, but no bathroom. That came later. They still used an "outhouse," but it was a "two-holer". They moved into their new home on May 30, 1946, and it was a mansion compared to the "pole" house on the Bluff.

Drawing of a "Pole House" of the period.

FROM CONNER LANDING
TO EUREKA LANDING

The distance from Conner Landing to Eureka Landing is 31 miles by the river. During the days of the Steamboats and the Daylight Line Boats, there were 19 landings between Conner Landing and Eureka Landing where the boats would stop at various times to pick up freight and/or passengers. Today, only three or four would be recognized as landings. All the others, including Conner Landing, have grown over with brush and trees. It's a shame that the old landings were not marked with signs to show where they once were located.

In the 1930s and 1940s one would often see barges being towed from Moss Bluff to Palatka.

A barge, sometimes as large as 20 feet wide and 60 feet long, would be expertly maneuvered around sharp bends in the river by experienced river men who had worked on the river most of their lives. It typically took about a week to take a barge to Palatka and return the towboat to Moss Bluff. Also seen floating downstream were log rafts. The logs were simply banded together and floated downriver to one of the lumber mills located on the St. Johns River.

We have now completed our journey down the Ocklawaha. We hope you have enjoyed your trip *"Around The Next Bend."*

Turpentine Industry

During the Steamboat Era on the Ocklawaha River, the turpentine industry was a key factor in keeping the riverboats plying the river. Its history may be as colorful as the steamboat era itself.

The production of naval stores, along with logging and lumbering, were the first major industries of the southern pine forests. The turpentine industry extracted resin from pine trees and distilled it to produce rosin, turpentine, pitch, tar, and other products. Over the past three centuries, naval stores were used in the construction of ships, paper sizing, and the manufacture of perfumes, adhesives, pharmaceutical supplies, plastics and paints.

Like other forest products, the naval stores industry provided employment for blacks leaving the plantation system during the Reconstruction Era. Archaeological investigations of the plantation system have provided glimpses of its social and economic nature. The lumber and turpentine industry was essentially an extension of the plantation system in that the relationships between the workers (slaves or indentured servants), the plantation owner, and the overseer remained essentially the same.

Over the years, due to the isolation of its workers, the turpentine industry evolved a distinct society, including lifestyle and language. It was even viewed as picturesque. A typical day's work for a turpentiner was from "kin to kant" (dawn to dark). He would rise about 4:30 a.m., eat a quick meal prepared the night before, and head into the woods at first light.

Between 8:00 and 9:00 a.m. the turpentiners ate a light meal which was also prepared and packed the night before. They worked until nearly sundown, then walked back to their quarters for supper and home chores. This ritual was performed five or six days per week depending on how fast each got his prescribed job done.

Woodsrider watching the work in a turpentine stand.

As in the plantation system, naval stores operations also had an overseer or foreman. This individual, who made his rounds on horseback, was called a "woodsrider". Woodsriders were generally caucasian and their duties were to inspect and supervise the work at a turpentine stand. The black workers were under the complete control of the woodsrider. In fact, it was said that the woodsrider, sporting a pistol and whip, was the law in those isolated areas.

The workers usually received company scrip or metal tokens as wages. These were only redeemable at the operator's commissary which was usually located at the turpentine distillery. Other forms of money could be acquired by trading the script at a discount, however, for most workers, access to areas outside the turpentine camp or distillery was forbidden. Saturday was generally payday at the turpentine camp. Male workers were paid about $10.00 per month, while female workers received about $8.00. The woodsrider, however, received around $30.00 per month, which was usually paid in real currency rather than script.

Goods were usually purchased on credit from the commissary whose keeper affixed a high interest charge. Thus, the workers were usually indebted to the company store, making their ability to leave the turpentine camps for other employment even less likely. The commodities supplied by the commissary system suggested that most meals of the workers probably consisted of cornbread, bacon, black coffee, and an occasional treat of baking powder biscuits. Local game and

fish were no doubt taken as so-called leisure time became available. Berries, grapes, persimmons, nuts, and other edible wild plant life were probably also gathered in season.

Housing and water were furnished as part of the workers compensation. Because the trees began to lose their productivity after several years, turpentine camps were occupied temporarily, usually for a period of five years. Most of the early trees were worked near rivers for easy shipment. Side camps and distilleries, where the resin was processed into turpentine, began moving into the interior portions of the forest when railroad lines were completed in the late 19th century.

Most turpentine workers lived in shacks or quarters grouped closely together or in rows to prevent the social isolation inherent in living alone in the woods, and to provide better means of overseeing and controlling workers activities. These rough lumber shanties, occupied by both workers and the woodsrider, were located at the side camps and at the distillery.

Early shanties for the workers were often one-room pole structures with no floor or windows. If a worker's family was large, a lean-to was often added along one wall for additional sleeping space. Each shanty occupant or family probably had a small garden of vegetables to supplement their diet.

Data compiled during a land acquisition appraisal of a Liberty County turpentine camp in the 1930s provides information on camp organization. The camp encompassed 640 acres (one square mile), and within its borders was found 27 box and frame quarters for 157 occupants and their families. The camp also included a combination church and school, commissary, and cemetery.

With few exceptions, archaeological remains from occupational areas of the side camp differ little from those of the distillery site, since most commodities at both types of sites were purchased at the company commissary. Glass and ceramic remains constitute the majority of the utilitarian materials associated with these sites. Kerosene lantern globes and bases, beverage and medicinal bottles, and ornate cut-glass are the most common types of glass artifacts reflecting life at the turpentine site. The greatest percentage of utilitarian ceramics collected from these sites is ironstone, with other types in lesser frequencies. The material remains associated with a turpentine stand include isolated objects such as beverage bottles, cups, tools, and other equipment used during the operation of gum collection, as well as an occasional domestic item.

The socio-economic conditions of turpentine workers remained constant, despite a number of technological advances which improved harvesting and processing techniques. One of the major developments which drastically changed the industry was the introduction of the clay collecting cup.

Initially, the gum or resin was collected in "boxes" or collecting basins chopped into the bases of trees with a broadaxe. A "streak" or wedge-shaped grove was cut into the face of the tree above the box to allow gum to flow. Each week a new streak was cut to increase this flow. The box cavity was found to weaken the tree at the base, leaving it vulnerable to disease, wind, and fire, and to lessen the value of the tree as timber for lumber.

Although the boxing method remained in common use until 1915, Charles Herty's 1904 invention of the clay cup initiated a new method for collecting pine resin. A streak was made in the tree and then an incision was cut into the face where a gutter was fastened to direct the flow of resin into the collect-

Major ownership in the Herty Cup Company was with the Consolidated Naval Stores Company of Jacksonville from 1910 until 1942 when the company was voluntarily dissolved. These dates correspond nicely with the major era of naval stores production in Florida, particularly in the Jacksonville area.

Another variety of clay collecting cups was connected to the tree by a metal fastener at the rim instead of being hung by a nail. A clay cup curved to fit the shape of the tree was also on the market during the final quarter of the 19th century. Although the location of manufacture is presently unknown, a patent date of July 10, 1910 is indicated on the bases of some of these cups.

Several varieties of yellow clay cups were apparently being made and used almost exclusively in the Escambia County, Florida area during the early 1930s. Although their paste was consistent, shapes and sizes varied greatly suggesting temporal distinctions in the styles or perhaps different manufactures. An unnamed Jacksonville company, possibly associated with Charles Herty's business, manufactured a cement cup in the mid 1930s. Experimental glass cups were also made in Jacksonville during the late 1930s.

As early as 1914, galvanized iron cups were on the market. Styles included the flowerpot shaped Birdeye cup, the trapezoid shaped Buzzard wing cup, and a variety of metal oblong boxes. During the 1920s and 1930s, an array of tin, galvanized iron, and aluminum cups were being manufactured for use in collecting pine resin. In a final attempt to produce quality resin, free of leaf litter and other debris, steel oblong boxes with a fired enamel finish were used during the waning years of the industry.

Herty clay cup used for resin collection.

ing cup which was hung in place below the gutter by a single nail. The use of clay increased the quality of resin by avoiding many of the impurities which tended to collect in the open box cavity.

The Museum of Florida History in Tallahassee has an extensive collection of turpentine cups which beautifully illustrate variations in 20th century clay and metal cups. Clay cups were almost exclusively used in Florida because they were much cheaper to purchase than metal, except in the northern part of the state where clay cups could easily break during a freeze.

The Herty cup was the most common style on the market. Established in 1904, the Herty Turpentine Cup Company of Daisy, Tennessee, produced at least 60,000 cups per day until about 1914, when the advent of galvanized iron cups forced a decrease in the demand for ceramic cups. These cups were marketed exclusively in Alabama, Georgia, and Florida.

Workers collecting turpentine resin and pitch.

Another source of data for establishing a chronology of the naval stores industry in Florida, is the development of specialized tools used in chopping and dipping the pine gum. Five technological innovations occurred in the industry between 1700 and 1865. Most of the changes that occurred in the industry's peak years between 1900 and 1935 were in collecting cups, but during the latter 50 years of the industry, at least 38 new tools, equipment, and extraction methods were adopted and accepted, over half of which occurred between 1942 and 1958.

The common chipping tool known as a hack replaced axes and single bevel hatchets in the first half of the 19th century. Further advancements were made in design during the early 20th century with the introduction of the No. 2 hack in 1900, the No. 0 hack in 1910, and the detachable blade hack in 1915. These early hacks, which were attached to a handle and weight, continued in use throughout the course of the industry.

To accompany the new extraction methods, a broadaxe for mauling the incision into the streak was introduced in 1908 to replace the boxing axe in use since 1700. A puller, invented in 1865 to chip high streaks, was still in use in the late 1930s.

In 1918, the hogal was invented to smooth the bark for gutter insertion and to chip subsequent streaks. Chipping paddles, to prevent chips from falling into the cup, were introduced during the late 1920s. Scrape boxes and various styles of scraping tools were also in use as early as the latter 1920s. Two styles of specialized buckets and dip paddles were invented in the 1930s to replace the dip spoon previously in use since 1750.

Naval stores and the turpentine industry were reliant on riverboat transportation to move and sell their products. The Ocklawaha River system was the only "highway" from interior forests to the cities until the late 1800s. Supplies needed to collect and process resin including axes, chipping tools, hatchets, collecting cups (in their various forms), as well as commissary supplies and other essentials for the workers were transported by riverboats to dozens of sites along the river. Riverboats sustained and promoted economic growth through the naval stores and turpentine industries along the Ocklawaha River.

Rectangular galvanized resin collection bucket.

Large turpentine still located near the Ocklawaha River.

Barrels waiting to be shipped.

Timber being processed for manufacturing barrels.

Workers returning after a hard day's work.

Firewood for processing turpentine at the still.

Workers returning after a hard day's work.

Workers making barrels to ship product.

DIORAMA OF A TURPENTINE STILL

Workers making barrels to ship product.

Worker scrapes resin into barrel for transport.

Each barrel is individually built by the cooper and used during the turpentine process.

Preparing the turpentine for the distilling process. This was hard work and required several men.

Turpentine collected from the trees "catface" and clay cups being emptied by workers.

Workers of all ages were used to work in the turpentine fields. They learned from an early age.

Log Rafting on the Ocklawaha River

"Pull boats" were an important part of the early lumber industry. The Wilson Cypress Company of Palatka, Florida, located on the St. Johns River, used pull boats to harvest logs from interior forests along the Ocklawaha River. The pull boat remained along the river's edge while workmen ran cables into the swamp. After a tree was cut down, the cables were fastened to the log, and it was pulled into the river. Then the workmen returned to the swamp for another log. This continued until there were a good many logs collected at the river's edge. They were then fastened together into a long "raft" of logs.

In the early days, they were moved along the river with long poles handled by river men. It took days to get them to Palatka. After delivering the logs, the river men had to walk back through the swamps to return home. Later these log rafts were towed by boats, which made the trip much quicker and easier. The pine logs were carried to the Browning Lumber Company and the cypress logs were taken to the Wilson Cypress Company lumber yard for processing.

Log rafting on the Ocklawaha River. Log rafts were fastened together by a cross log on each end, then the individual rafts are placed in tandem using a single pole as a hinge, this enables the rafts to make sharp river bends. Steering is done with long push poles with possibly a "rudder" on the lead raft.

Lumber Industry

Mules with carts were used in the lumber yards to move the timber around for cutting.

Timber after being floated down river waiting to be cut.

Timber being inspected before cutting.

Trees being marked for cutting by a woodsman.

Worker resting after a hard day of cutting cypress.

Logs being inspected and graded before cutting.

Logs being cut into lumber boards in the mill.

Workers with a full lumber yard of product.

Citrus Industry

One of the most important commodities to be transported by the riverboats was citrus. Oranges, grapefruit, and tangerines were shipped north, and in the early years they were transported in closed barrels. It was discovered that the citrus remained fresher if shipped in an open crate container. As the industry grew, packing houses developed colorful crate labels which advertised Florida. citrus and their businesses.

The largest citrus grove located on the Ocklawaha River was at Conner Landing. It was approximately 11+ acres in size, growing several types of citrus such as naval oranges, white and pink grapefruit, and tangerines. Tourists enjoyed stopping at the landing and picking fresh citrus to take with them on their trip.

The citrus industry flourished in the early years, and the once large groves diminished in size over the years due to severe freezes and land development.

Samples of crate labels of the period.

Plentiful crop of oranges being picked.

Profitable crop being picked for shipment.

A young worker enjoys fruits of his labors.

Grove workers harvesting the crop.

Citrus grove picking crew.

Often entire families worked together in the groves to earn income for their families. The grove workers worked long, hard hours gathering fruit, also contributing to the economic development of the area.

Profitable crop being picked for shipment.

A busy day of picking fruit.

Mature citrus trees with a bountiful harvest.

A train with tourists going through a citrus grove.
Many times they would stop for fresh fruit.

A large grove located near the Ocklawaha River with owner's home in background.

Some say we had the "biggest and best" fruit in the world.

Early packing house where fruit was checked and placed in crates for shipping.

As the industry progressed, more ways of processing the fruit were devised.

Early Ocala

A few miles west of Silver Springs lies the City of Ocala, which is the county seat for Marion County. Ocala was greatly influenced by riverboat traffic and the many tourists that visited the area. In the early years, it was considered an adventure to travel up the Ocklawaha River and experience the beauty and ambiance of it.

Many times, tourists came and returned home with their memories, but often they stayed and created new lives here. Ocala has grown through the years and has become one of Florida's unique cities, drawing many to its lifestyle.

"Lovers Lane" in the early days of Ocala.

Horse-drawn carts on early Ocala downtown street.

On Main Street looking south.

Horses on Broadway Street at the square.

Harrington Hall Hotel east of the downtown square.

The train depot was a busy place in the early days.

Train station where many visitors came to visit Ocala.

United States Post Office and the Hotel Marion in the background located on Magnolia Avenue.

Looking north on Magnolia Avenue from the square.

Hotel Marion located on Magnolia Avenue.

Marion County Court House and gazebo. View from the corner of Broadway and Main Streets.

Corner of Main Street and Ocklawaha Blvd. (E. Hwy. 40)

Hotel Ocala, formerly Harrington Hall Hotel.

Looking east downtown on Broadway Street.

A beautiful home located on East Ft. King Street.

Ocala has a rich history of golfing by locals and tourists.

Early high school located in downtown Ocala.

In the late 1800s and early 1900s, when steamboats churned the Ocklawaha River and Ocala's streets echoed with the sound of wagon wheels, paper money often carried the name of the town itself. Local banks—such as The Ocala National Bank and The Munroe and Chambliss National Bank—issued their own currency under the National Banking Acts. These notes were printed by skilled engravers in Philadelphia or New York, then signed by Ocala's own bank officers before entering circulation. Farmers, merchants, and riverboat captains alike handled them daily, folding them into oilskin pouches or tucking them into account ledgers. With intricate scrollwork, portraits of statesmen, and bold lettering proclaiming "Ocala, Florida," they were as much a symbol of civic confidence as they were a medium of exchange. Today, they survive as tangible reminders of a time when money looked—and felt—like a piece of local history.

Above, obverse of a $20 1902 The Ocala National Bank bank note. *Below,* obverse and reverse of a $10 1902 The Munroe and Chambliss National Bank bank note.

RIVERBOAT LANDING

Scrapbook

A collection of images
of riverboats and the
Ocklawaha River.

Man in a cypress dugout canoe
poling his way downstream on
the Ocklawaha River with a
riverboat in the background.

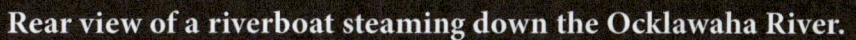

Rear view of a riverboat steaming down the Ocklawaha River.

Hiawatha nearing Eureka Landing.

Riverboat on the beautiful Ocklawaha River.

The William Howard at Eureka Landing.

Egrets and alligators were abundant along the river.

Spanish moss hanging over the peaceful Ocklawaha River.

Chief Osceola's Old Field Landing.

Hiawatha riverboat passengers view the many marvels of the river.

View of the Hiawatha as it plyed the Ocklawaha River. Note the "fire box" on the top of the riverboat; it provided the only illumination for navigation and nightime travel.

Photo Credits

79 - stereo, FPC

80 - Upper, Rambler, *A Guide to Florida*, 1875 – Lower, Bicaise, *A Guide to the Land of Flowers*, 1878, Mueller collection

81 - George Barker photo, 1886, Mueller collection

82 - Upper, George Barker photo, 1886, Mueller collection – Lower, Ocala Historical Society, FPC

83 - Upper, stereo, FPC – Lower, C. Bradford Mitchell collection

84 - Upper, C. Bradford Mitchell – Lower, George Barker, Niagara Falls, N. Y. photo, Robert Cauthen collection, FPC

85 - Upper, C. Bradford Mitchell - Lower, E. Bien and Company photo (Palatka), FPC

86 - C. Bradford Mitchell collection

87 - C. Bradford Mitchell collection

88 - Upper, old post card, Mueller collection – Lower, C. Bradford Mitchell collection

89 - C. Bradford Mitchell collection

90 - Upper, C. Bradford Mitchell collection – Lower, Mueller collection

91 - Upper, Health Resorts of the South, 1884 – Lower, Bicaise, *A Guide to the Land of Flowers*, 1878

92 - Upper, Havens photo "On the Ocklawaha – Sunlight Pictures," 1885, FPC – Lower, C. Bradford Mitchell collection

93 - Upper and lower, Mueller collection

94 - Mueller collection

95 - Courtesy artist Ed Jonas

96 - Mueller collection

97 - Upper, Lewis of Palatka photo, John Palmer loan, FPC – Lower, Detroit Photographic Co., 1902 "On the Ocklawaha"

98 - C. Bradford Mitchell collection

99 - Upper, Florida State University – Lower, *Leve and Alden's Guide*, 1880

100 - Tickets, courtesy Florida Archives

101 - 109 - Mueller collection

110 - 111 - Mueller collection

112 - 113 - Mueller collection

114 - Eldredge collection Mariners Museum

115 - Upper, Eldredge collection, Mariners Museum – Lower, Mueller collection

116 - Upper, stereo, Mueller collection – Lower Eldredge collection Mariners Museum

117 - Upper, Mueller collection – Lower, Kilburn stereo #580, FPC

118 - Upper, Robert Cauthen collection, FPC – Lower, P. K. Yonge Library collection, University of Florida, Gainesville

119 - Both photos, John Palmer loan, FPC

120 - C. Bradford Mitchell collection

121 - C. Bradford Mitchell collection

122 - Upper, HAMMS collection, Smithsonian – Lower, Mueller collection

123 - HAMMS collection, Smithsonian, also Florida Archives

124 - Author

125 - Upper, Highways and Byways of Florida, 1918 Lower, Albertype collection

126 - C. Bradford Mitchell collection

127 - Old post cards, Mueller collection

128 - Upper, C. W. Stoll collection taken in April, 1917 – Lower, Mueller collection

129 - Upper, Florida State News Bureau, Tallahassee – Lower, Al Robson photo, FPC

130 - HAMMS collection, Smithsonian, also Florida Archives

136 - Mueller collection

137 - Upper, Mueller collection – Lower, post card, Mueller collection

138 - Upper, Captain Henry Hamment, FPC – Lower post card, courtesy W. Brand, FPC

139 - Mueller collection

140 - Both, courtesy of Kenneth Merrill

141 - Florida Archives

142 - Both photos, Caroline Wellhoner Farmer, FPC

143 - Upper, HAMMS collection, Smithsonian - Lower, Mueller collection

Note: SRMC is an acronym for Silver River Museum
Collection located in Ocala, Florida.

145 - Michael C. Mason collection
146 - Mason Family collection
147 - All Photos SRMC
148 - FPC
149 - SRMC
150 - FPC
152 - Upper: SRMC, Peake Album, FPC
153 - Upper: Mason Family collection, Lower:
William Carl Mason
154 - All Photographs, Mason Family collection
155 - Mason Family collection
156 - Michael C. Mason collection
157 - Upper & Lower: Mason Family collection
158 - Mason Family collection
159 - Mason Family collection
160 - Upper & Lower: Mason Family collection
161 - Mason Family collection
162 - Line Drawing by Dale Eric Mason
163 - SRMC
164 - Michael C. Mason collection
165 - Michael C. Mason collection
166 - Upper: Photo by Michael C. Mason – Lower:
Michael C. Mason collection
167 - Upper photo by Michael C. Mason, Lower:
Michael C. Mason collection
168 - All Photos: US Forestry Department

169 - All Photos: Michael C. Mason
170 - Upper: Mason Family collection, Lower: Both
Photos, FPC
171 - Michael C. Mason collection
172 - Both Photos: US Forestry Department
173 - All Photos: US Forestry Department
174 - Upper: SRMC, Both Lower: Cynthia L Plesner
Crate Label collection
175 - All Photos: Mason Family collection
176 - Mason Family collection
177 - Mason Family collection
178 - Michael C. Mason collection
179 - SRMC
180 - SRMC
181 - Mason Family collection
182 - Mason Family collection
183 - Michael C. Mason collection
184 - Heritage Auctions, ha.com - bank notes in
personal collection of Carl Plesner
185 - Michael C. Mason collection
186 - Michael C. Mason collection
187 - Michael C. Mason collection
188 - Michael C. Mason collection
189 - Michael C. Mason collection
196 - Photo by Stephen F. Rawls

Footnotes

[1] Raymond and Whitcomb pamphlet, *A Series of Delightful Tours Through Florida*, 1897.

[2] Annual Reports, War Dept. FY 1919, Report of the Chief of Engineers, U.S. Army 1919. Part I Wash. GPO 1919, p 789.

[3] Ibid.

[4] Ibid.

[5] Brinton, Daniel, *Notes of the Florida Peninsula* (Philadelphia), 1859, p 184.

[6] Ibid.

[7] Jacksonville News, August 5, 1854.

[8] Undated correspondence from W. J. Winegar to Dr. A. J. Hanna, Rollins College Collection (Winegar was Hart's son-in-law)

[9] Information about Captain Gray largely derived from a private publication (1922) by his son, Edward Wurtz Gray, hereinafter referred to as Gray.

[10] Cabell, Branch and A. J. Hanna, *The St. Johns, A Parade of Diversities* (New York: Farrar and Rinehart, 1943), p 252.

[11] List of Merchant Vessels of the United States, 1868, Washington, D.C., 1868. (All vessel dimensions, official number and data, subsequently shown, are derived from various annual issues of this publication).

[12] Gray

[13] Ibid.

[14] Ibid.

[15] Davis, William Watson, *The Civil War and Reconstruction in Florida*, New York, Columbia University Press, 1913, p 198.

[16] Mitchell, C. Bradford, "Paddle-Wheel Inboard", *The American Neptune*, Vol. VII (1947), two issues, April and July, 1947, p 122. Hereinafter cited as Mitchell.

[17] Ibid, p 122.

[18] Ibid, p 123.

[19] Gray. The following relates to Gray's slaves.

One of Captain Gray's slaves, "Daddy Mark," was left at Palatka to care for the Gray house. Accused of burning a house, along with two white men, he was hanged. The Gray family believed him innocent of the crime. His wife, Mauma, was the nurse for the young Gray children and moved to Savannah after the war. They had two children, Ben and Henry. Another slave, Jack, was a deck hand on Captain Gray's steamboat. He was an accomplished musician and played homemade instruments he constructed from materials on hand. He was carried away on a Union gunboat but returned after the war with a trunk full of presents for the Gray children. Other slaves were Dennis Cooper, who was bought for $2,000 from the Sanchez family; he was the yard man in Palatka and cared for the livestock there. The cook was Sarah who had an awful temper and at times would run Mrs. Gray out of the kitchen. Captain Gray calmed her down by hiring her out. Two slaves, Elsie and Lydia, were sisters. Lydia had five children which Captain Gray bought at Elsie's request. Two other slaves, Dan and Ben Singleton, ran away on a federal vessel to Hilton Head. Dan returned after the war but not Ben. Another slave, George Washington, was a faithful deck hand.

A son of Captain Gray, Edward Wurtz Gray, says that the Grays never punished, "nor permitted the punishment of any of their slaves." They also never punished their children. "An unruly child was told to get a slate, sit in the corner and copy a few pages of history. That was sufficient, especially when it occurred during 'play' time."

[20] Ibid.

[21] Mitchell, p 125.

[22] Ibid, p 128.

[23] Minutes of the Proceedings of the Board of Trustees of the Internal Improvement Fund of the State of Florida, Volume 1, Florida State Printer, 1902. March 5, 1866 Board Meeting. Minutes hereinafter cited as Trustees.

[24] Ibid.

[25] Ibid, October 26, 1867.

[26] Ibid.

[27] Ibid, January 14, 1868.

[28] Ibid, March 13, 1868.

[29] Ibid, August 31, 1868.

[30] Ibid, February 4, 1869.

[31] Mitchell, p 128.

[32] Ibid, p 129.

[33] Ibid, p 129.

[34] Ibid, p 131.

[35] Trustees, February 4, 1869.

[36] Mitchell, p 132.

[37] Ibid, p 132.

[38] Ibid, p 132

[39] Ibid, p 143

[40] Brinton, Daniel, *A Guide-book of Florida and the South*, Philadelphia, 1869, pp 88-90.

[41] Ibid, pp 91-92.

[42] Mitchell, p 138.

[43] Ibid, p 140.

[44] (Unsigned), "The Ocklawaha", *Harpers New Monthly Magazine*, January, 1876, Volume 52, pp 161-179 in part.

[45] Bicaise, *A Guide to the Land of Flowers*, 1878.

[46] *Florida Union*, November 20, 1881.

[47] Mitchell, p 135.

[48] Ibid, p 136.

[49] Ibid, p 141.

[50] Printed information listed on reverse of stereo card, dated February, 1881, author's collection.

[51] *Harpers Weekly*, Volume 24, 1880, p 110.

[52] Advertisement in pamphlet, printed by the South Georgia, Florida, Savannah and Western Railway Company, 1882, "*A Brief Description and how to Reach There.*"

[53] Advertisement in *Southern Business Advertizer*, 1879.

[54] Mitchell, C. Bradford, WAUNITA notes typescript data.

[55] *Florida Union*, January 13, 1882.

[56] *Florida Union*, November 20, 1881 (advertisement).

[57] *Florida Union*, November 20, 1881.

[58] Mitchell, C. Bradford, typescript of vessel enrollment data.

[59] *Florida Union*, January 18 date of advertisement, February 1 issue, 1882.

[60] *Florida Union*, February 3 date of advertisement, February 25 issue, 1882.

[61] Ibid, December 20, 1881.

[62] Mitchell, p 127, 128.

[63] Undated brochure, "*Rules for the Hart Line of Ocklawaha River Steamers.*"

[64] Mitchell, p 153, 154.

[65] Ibid, p 142, 143, 144.

[66] Ibid, p 153.

[67] Hardy, Iza Duffus, *Oranges and Alligators, Sketches of South Florida Life*, London, pp 134, 135, 137, 138, 140.

[68] Invoices, dated April 8, 9, 1896 from A. M. Haughton and Bro., Palatka, Florida, Florida State Archives.

[69] Mitchell, p 158, 159.

[70] Ibid, p 160.

[71] Ibid, p 163, 165.

[72] Bicaise, "*Guide to the Land of Flowers*", 1878.

[73] Mitchell, p 163, 164.

[74] Ibid, p 140 (in part).

[75] Schedule cards, Hart Line, Lucas Line, advertised in the *Standard Guide*, St. Augustine, 1895.

[76] Mitchell, p 166.

[77]Gray (His wife survived him by 22 years. His sons, Harry and Edward, served with him on his boats).

[78]Mitchell, p 224.

[79]Ibid, p 225.

[80]Mitchell p 226, quoting Swift, F. R., *Florida Fancies*, p 41, 43.

[81]Mitchell, p 231.

[82]Correspondence to author, dated July 8, 1964.

[83]Mitchell, p 235.

[84]Silver Springs Transportation Company brochure, *"Florida Daylight Route, Ocklawaha River, 1917"*.

[85]Mitchell, p 236.

[86]Ibid, p 239.

About the Authors

Edward A. Mueller (1932–2014)

Edward A. Mueller was a respected maritime historian and author whose passion for steamboats and inland waterways shaped decades of research and writing. Based in Florida, Mueller dedicated much of his life to documenting the rich heritage of steamboat travel throughout the southeastern United States.

His interest in steamboats and steamships, predominantly those associated with Florida, continued for over five decades. He collected photographs and written materials about steam vessels and researched subjects of interest to him and, as the occasion permitted, published historical written and pictorial accounts on such subjects.

He authored numerous books and articles on steamboating, including definitive works on the St. Johns River, the Suwannee River, and Florida's Gulf Coast, and was widely recognized for his meticulous attention to historical accuracy, archival research, and rare image curation. *Ocklawaha River Steamboats* remains one of his most celebrated titles, capturing the romance and history of one of Florida's most mysterious and storied waterways.

Mueller's prior works also appeared in periodicals such as the *Florida Historical Quarterly*, *Tequesta*, *Jacksonville Seafarer*, *Nautical Research Journal*, *The Reflector*, *The Weather Gauge*, and *Steamboat Bill*. He gave many lectures and slide presentations on nautical subjects. He published many other books on nautical subjects.

Mueller served in the U.S. Navy Seabees in World War II (retired as a Lieutenant-Commander, USNR). While in government service, he was the Executive Director of the Jacksonville Transportation Authority for eight years and the initial Secretary of the Florida Department of Transportation.

Mueller was a member of Lions Clubs International for many years, serving his club and community.

Michael C. Mason (1951–2014)

Michael C. Mason had an interest in Ocklawaha riverboats for many years, collecting images, artifacts, and information. In 1989, he developed a mobile display unit, and he and his father traveled throughout north central Florida to many schools and events showing images and memorabilia and telling stories about the Ocklawaha River and its riverboats.

Mason was an Aerial Combat Photographer in the United States Air Force. He served in Southeast Asia photographing the war effort in Thailand, Vietnam, Burma, Cambodia, and Laos. He had air time in both fixed winged and rotor aircraft and 118 combat missions aboard the Phantom F-4.

Mason had been a member of Lions Clubs International from 1973 until his passing and served as District Governor of Florida's 35L, 2007- 2008, and Counsel Chairman of Multiple District 35, Florida and the Bahamas, 2008-2009.

Mason and Mueller were friends for many years, sharing a joint interest in riverboats and the Ocklawaha River. Mason agreed to include portions of Mueller's book, *Ocklawaha River Steamboats*, in this *Riverboat Landing* book.